Twenty-Five Lessons

in

CITIZENSHIP

D. L. HENNESSEY

Citizenship Teacher and Director of Adult Education,
Berkeley, California

Citizenship Department, Evening High School of Commerce,
San Francisco, California

Supervisor of Citizenship Classes,
Northern California

Revised by
LENORE HENNESSEY RICHARDSON

NINETY-SIXTH EDITION
1991-1992

"Give me your tired, your poor,
Your huddled masses yearning to breathe free,
The wretched refuse of your teeming shore.
Send these, the homeless, tempest-tost to me,
I lift my lamp beside the golden door."

Inscription on the Statue of Liberty

BERKELEY, CALIFORNIA

Copyright © 1991 by Lenore Hennessey Richardson

ISBN 1-879773-00-7

CONTENTS

SPECIAL REFERENCES

GETTYSBURG ADDRESS
Delivered by President Abraham Lincoln
at Gettysburg, Pennsylvania, November 19, 1863

Four score and seven years ago our fathers brought forth on this continent a new nation, conceived in liberty and dedicated to the proposition that all men are created equal.

Now we are engaged in a great civil war, testing whether that nation or any nation so conceived and so dedicated can long endure. We are met on a great battlefield of that war. We have come to dedicate a portion of that field, as a final resting-place of those who here gave their lives that that nation might live. It is altogether fitting and proper that we should do this.

But, in a larger sense, we cannot dedicate—we cannot consecrate—we cannot hallow—this ground. The brave men, living and dead, who struggled here, have consecrated it, far above our poor power to add or detract. The world will little note, nor long remember, what we say here, but it can never forget what they did here. It is for us the living, rather, to be dedicated here to the unfinished work which they who fought here have thus far so nobly advanced. It is rather for us to be here dedicated to the great task remaining before us—that from these honored dead we take increased devotion to that cause for which they gave the last full measure of devotion—that we here highly resolve that these dead shall not have died in vain—that this nation, under God, shall have a new birth of freedom—and that government of the people, by the people, for the people shall not perish from the earth.

LESSON I

CITIZENSHIP

A new immigration law was enacted in 1990. The law will increase overall immigration from 540,000 in 1989 to 700,000 people a year for each of the next three years and stabilize the annual total at 675,000 after that.

It changes the 1950s-era immigration ban against Communists and homosexuals but would still allow the secretary of state discretion to bar legal status to those considered to be terrorists or foreign policy threats.

The law will also:

Allow more people to immigrate on the basis of desirable employment skills, reserving 140,000 visas a year for immigrants with special skills, up from 54,000 in the past.

Give special status to wealthy investors, setting aside 10,000 visas for those with at least $500,000 to invest in businesses that create new jobs.

Eliminate the automatic exclusion of AIDS patients from legal status. The legislation leaves it up to the Health and Human Services Department to decide whether to list AIDS as an excludable disease.

Earmark 40,000 visas a year for individuals from Italy, Poland, Ireland and other countries virtually shut off from immigration in the past 20 years because priority was given to people with family here, most of whom were from Asian and Latin countries.

Reserve at least 16,000 of those 40,000 visas a year for Irish immigrants, making Ireland the only country with a guaranteed number of visas.

Grant a special "temporary protected status" until July 1992 to Salvadorans. For several years, Salvadorans fleeing domestic violence, including right-wing death squads, have waged a struggle against deportation.

Allow for naturalization of Filipinos who served in the U.S. military or Philippine Army or guerrilla units in World War II.

Expedite deportation of aliens convicted of criminal activities and grant general arrest authority to the Immigration and Naturalization Service.

Non-quota visas will be available to husbands, wives and unmarried children of United States citizens or resident aliens and to parents of adult United States citizens. Not more than 20,000 persons, however, may be admitted from any one country in any given year.

The Immigration and Naturalization Service prepares and issues regulations in connection with all of the Immigration and Naturalization Laws. Any person having a problem involving a peculiar point of Naturalization or Immigration Law should request an official opinion from the Immigration and Naturalization Service office nearest him. Immigration and Naturalization Service offices are to be found at the following locations:

Anchorage, Alaska, 99501, U.S. Post Office and Courthouse Building, Room 142

Atlanta, Ga., 30309, 881 Peachtree Street NE

Baltimore, Md., 21202, 707 North Calvert Street

Boston, Mass., 02111, 150 Tremont Street

Buffalo, N.Y., 14202, 68 Court Street

Chicago, Ill., 60607, 932 Post Office Building, 433 West Van Buren Street

Cleveland, Ohio, 44113, 600 Standard Building, 1370 Ontario Street

Denver, Colo., 80202, 437 Post Office Building

Detroit, Mich., 48207, 3770 East Jefferson Avenue

El Paso, Tex., 79984, 343 U.S. Courthouse

Frankfurt, Germany, c/o American Consulate General

Hartford, Conn., 06101, 135 High Street

Helena, Mont., 59601, Federal Building

Honolulu, Hawaii 96809, 595 Ala Moana Boulevard

Kansas City, Mo., 64106, 819 U.S. Courthouse, 811 Grand Avenue

Los Angeles, Calif., 90012, 300 North Los Angeles Street

Manila, Philippine Islands, c/o American Embassy

Mexico City, Mexico, c/o American Embassy, Mexico, D.F., Mexico

Miami, Fla., 33130, Room 1402, Federal Building, 51 Southwest First Avenue

Newark, N.J., 07102, 1060 Broad Street

New Orleans, La., 70113, New Federal Building, 701 Loyola Avenue

New York, N.Y., 10007, 20 West Broadway

Omaha, Nebr., 68102, New Federal Building, 215 North 17th Street

Philadelphia, Pa., 19102, 128 North Broad Street

Phoenix, Ariz., 85025, 230 North First Avenue

Port Isabel, Tex., 78566, Route 3 Los Fresnos, Texas

Portland, Maine, 04112, 319 U.S. Courthouse

Portland, Ore., 97205, 333 U.S. Courthouse, Broadway and Main Street

Rome, Italy, c/o American Embassy

St. Albans, Vt., 05478, 45 Kingman Street

St. Paul, Minn., 55101, 1014 New Post Office Building, 180 East Kellogg Boulevard

San Antonio, Tex., 78206, U.S. Post Office and Courthouse

San Francisco, Calif., 94111, Appraisers Building, 630 Sansome Street

San Juan, P.R., 804 Ponce de Leon Avenue, Santurce, P.R., 00908

Seattle, Wash., 98134, 815 Airport Way, South

Washington, D.C., 20536, 311 Old Post Office Building, 12th and Pennsylvania Avenue NW

Many people confuse the words "citizen" and "voter." The two words have not the same meaning. A voter in this country must be a citizen of the United States, but not all citizens are voters. For example, all people born in the United States and subject to its jurisdiction are citizens of the United States, but they do not become voters until they reach the legal age.

Citizenship is one of the greatest privileges which the United States confers upon alien-born residents. This privilege is given through naturalization. The naturalization regulations are uniform throughout the nation.

4

NATURALIZATION OF REGULAR APPLICANTS

A. REQUIREMENTS

1. *Age*—The applicant must be eighteen years of age before a valid petition for naturalization may be filed.

2. *Lawful Entry*—The applicant must prove that he has been lawfully admitted to the United States for permanent residence. The Naturalization Service will verify the entry based upon information shown in the application form.

3. *Residence Requirements.*

a. Continuous residence in the "United States" (see Question 8) for at least five years preceding the date of filing of the petition.

b. Residence for at least six months immediately preceding the filing of the petition within the state in which the petition is filed.

c. Continuous residence in the United States from the date of the petition up to the time of admission to citizenship.

d. There is a difference between *residence* and *physical presence*. A person may be a *resident* of a place even though not *physically present* in that place at all times. The new naturalization law requires that the applicant prove that he has been *physically present* in the United States for at least half of the five-year period preceding the filing of his petition.

e. During the period for which continuous residence is required, an absence for more than six but less than twelve months will break the continuity of residence unless the applicant can prove that he did not intend to abandon his United States residence.

An absence of 365 days during residence will break the continuity of residence for naturalization purposes. Certain categories of aliens, defined in Section 316(b) may file form N-470 to preserve residence. Even if the alien meets the technical requirements the particular person must present the application prior to leaving the U.S. or before serving more than 365 days in employment abroad.

4. *Moral Character*—The applicant must be (1) of good moral character, (2) attached to the principles of the Constitution of the United States and (3) well disposed to the good order and happiness of the United States.

Some persons hesitate to apply for citizenship because at some time in their past they have committed a crime and were convicted for it. The law recognizes that people can and should be rehabilitated. If the person is a person of good moral character and has been such during the five years preceding the filing of his petition, the earlier conviction will not necessarily prevent the grant of citizenship.

5. *Racial Restrictions*—The law provides that the right to naturalization shall not be denied to a person because of his race. This means that aliens who were formerly ineligible to citizenship may now be naturalized. (See Question 4.)

6. *Language and Educational Requirements.*

a. The applicant must be able to read, write, and speak words in ordinary usage in the English language. However, this requirement is satisfied if he can read and write simple words. Normally an applicant can acquire enough English for this examination by attending citizenship classes. Most school districts conduct these classes as a part of the adult education program.

b. The language requirement does not apply to persons who are physically unable to comply with it if they are otherwise qualified. (For example, a blind person would not be required to read English.) Any alien who has attained the age of 50 and has been a lawful permanent resident of the U.S. for 20 years may claim an exemption from the literacy requirement. The 20 years need not be continuous, but only status as an immigrant (green card holder) counts. Those who have the above exemption may take the examination in their preferred language.

c. All applicants must take an examination showing knowledge of the history, principles, and government of the United States. Generally, the Naturalization Service provides interpreters for those who possess the above exemption.

B. PROCEDURE:

1. The alien must fill in a form entitled *"Application to File Petition for Naturalization"* (Form N-400) and mail or take same to the nearest Immigration and Naturalization Service Office. He must include with the form three identical front-view photographs of himself, 2″ x 2″ in size, taken against a light background, and not more than thirty days old. The alien must apply for naturalization in a court where he or she resides. (See Question 6.)

The name which the applicant signs to the application form should be his true and correctly spelled name, followed by any other name or other spelling which has been used at any time.

2. Upon receipt of the application form, the Naturalization Service conducts a preliminary check to verify the information given in the application regarding entry into the United States. Processing time will vary by office.

3.   After the entry has been verified, the Service will notify the applicant to appear at a specified time. At the time indicated the applicant will be questioned. The applicant is questioned as to all of the matters contained in his application form. Also, he may be examined at this time on his knowledge of the English language (unless exempt) and his knowledge of the history and principles of the United States government.

4.   Upon completion of the preliminary questioning, the applicant appears in person before the Clerk of the Naturalization Court (see Question 6). At this time the petition form is signed by the applicant and filed with the Clerk. The Clerk collects the filing fee of $50.00.

5.   The next step is the examination of the applicant. At this time he must show that he understands and speaks the English language (unless exempt) and that he has an understanding of the fundamental principles of the Constitution and some knowledge of the general history and ideals of the United States. He must satisfy the examiner that his character is good, and that he will be a loyal citizen of the United States. Procedure will vary somewhat depending on the Naturalization Court which has been selected.

6.   After all preliminary matters have been completed, the final hearing at court will be held. Waiting time varies.

The oath of allegiance is as follows:

OATH OF ALLEGIANCE

"I hereby declare, on oath, that I absolutely and entirely renounce and abjure all allegiance and fidelity to any foreign prince, potentate, state or sovereignty of whom or which I have heretofore been a subject or citizen; that I will support and defend the Constitution and the laws of the United States of America against all enemies, foreign and domestic; that I will bear true faith and allegiance to the same; that I will bear arms on behalf of the United States when required by law; that I will perform noncombatant service in the Armed Forces of the United States when required by the law; or that I will perform work of national importance under civilian direction when required by the law; and that I take this obligation freely without any mental reservation or purpose of evasion: SO HELP ME GOD . . . . ."

Considering the many thousands who take the oath of allegiance every year, the number of undesirable naturalized citizens is extremely small. The general attitude and response of naturalized citizens to the calls and needs of our government during war periods is especially gratifying. Many of our most public-spirited citizens are of foreign birth. Many first-generation descendants of naturalized citizens hold high and responsible positions in American public life. Among the prominent alien-born citizens of recent years may be mentioned Alexander Graham Bell, Samuel Gompers, James J. Hill, Jacob Riis, John Muir, Edward Bok, S. S. McClure, James Davis and Albert Einstein.

IMMIGRATION AND NATURALIZATION
OF SPECIAL CLASSES OF APPLICANTS

There are several groups of applicants for Immigration (entering the United States) and Naturalization (becoming citizens) to whom special laws apply. The rules vary in particular cases and definite information on any one of the classes can be obtained from the Immigration and Naturalization Services. Some of these special classes of applicants are as follows:

1. Husbands, wives, and unmarried children, of United States citizens or resident aliens and parents of adult United States citizens.
2. Former citizens of the United States regaining United States citizenship.
3. Aliens serving or who have served in the Armed Forces of the United States.
4. Refugees.
5. Aliens arriving in the United States before 1906.
6. Aliens who have served as crew men on United States vessels.

INFORMATION OF GENERAL INTEREST

1. *Declarations of Intention.*

It is no longer necessary to file a Declaration of Intention. However, some employers refuse to hire aliens unless they have declared their intention to become United States citizens. Under the law, any alien over 18 years who has been lawfully admitted to this country for permanent residence, may file an application on Form N-300 for declaration of intention to become a citizen. After that application has been approved by the Naturalization Service, the applicant will be notified to appear before the clerk of the Naturalization Court and sign Form N-315 which is the Declaration of Intention. The fee for this is $15.00. The declaration may be made at any time after lawful admission to this country for permanent residence.

2. *Aliens who cannot prove legal entry.*

a. The law provides special rules for aliens who entered the United States before July 1, 1924, but who cannot prove legal entry. In some cases these are people who entered the country illegally, such as deserters from foreign ships. In other cases, they are persons who may have entered legally, but whose records of entry cannot be found. Applicants in these groups must prove continuous United States residence since July 1, 1924, and must show themselves to be persons of good moral character. If they are able to satisfy these requirements and are not subject to deportation or otherwise ineligible to citizenship, a record of lawful admission for permanent residence can be established. Thereafter, these persons may proceed with the usual steps towards naturalization.

b. In 1986 the federal government passed a law that aliens who entered the U.S. before 1982 might apply for amnesty, if they did so by May 1988. Amnesty recipients who apply for permanent residency must either take a course from an INS certified school or pass an oral and written examination similar to the citizenship test. People who thereby gain permanent residency will receive a "green card" in the mail. The qualifications must be met by 31 months after the granting of amnesty.

QUESTIONS AND ANSWERS

1. Q. How long must an alien live in the United States before filing a petition for naturalization?

A. Unless he comes within a "special class," an alien must prove five years' residence in the United States and six months' residence in the state from which he applies. Both of these periods of residence must be immediately before the date of filing the petition. The new law requires him, in addition, to prove that he was physically present in the United States for at least one-half (thirty months) of the five year period.

2. Q. What are the other qualifications necessary for naturalization?

A. The ordinary applicant must be at least eighteen years old; he must prove that he has been lawfully admitted to the United States for residence; he must be of good moral character and attached to the principles of the United States Constitution and form of government; he must, unless exempt, be able to read, write, and speak words in ordinary use in the English language; he must pass an examination on the history, principles, ideals, and form of government of the United States.

3. **Q.** What is the citizenship status of people of Chinese, Japanese, Filipino and other Oriental descent who are born in the United States?
   A. They are citizens of the United States by right of birth. The United States Constitution guarantees them all the privileges of citizenship.

4. **Q.** Are any aliens ineligible to citizenship because of race?
   A. No. For many years American citizenship was denied to certain people, particularly those of Oriental descent. In December, 1943, properly qualified Chinese became eligible and substantial numbers of them have been naturalized since that date. In July, 1946, the ban with regard to Filipino persons was lifted. The 1952 law removed all racial barriers to naturalization.

5. **Q.** If their parents are not citizens, will children born in the United States be citizens?
   A. Yes. The United States Constitution provides that "All persons born or naturalized in the United States and subject to the jurisdiction thereof, are citizens of the United States and of the state wherein they reside."

6. **Q.** Which courts are "Naturalization Courts"?
   A. The following are Naturalization Courts:

   1. United States District Courts now existing or which may be established in any state, the District of Columbia, Puerto Rico, Guam, and the Virgin Islands.

   2. In addition to the above, certain state courts are authorized to conduct naturalization proceedings. In California, for example, the Superior Courts in each county may handle naturalization cases. In other states, it may be the County Court, the State District Court, or some other designated tribunal. It should be noted, however, that many of the state courts do not exercise their right to handle naturalization matters. In some, alien applicants for citizenship are referred in all cases to the Federal District Court nearest their place of residence.

7. **Q.** What are some of the advantages of being a citizen?
   A. A citizen can vote; he can hold office; he can sign petitions; he can take Civil Service Examinations; he can serve on juries; he can usually obtain better positions; he can engage in occupations from which aliens are excluded; he can share in many privileges and rights which

are granted to citizens only; he is guaranteed the protection of this government at home and abroad; if he wishes to visit any country outside the United States, he may obtain a passport which entitles him to the rights of an American citizen.

8. *Q.* The residence requirement of the naturalization law calls for five years' continuous residence in the United States. Does this mean that the applicant must have resided within one of the 50 states of the Union?
    A. No. "United States" as used in this law means the 50 states of the union *plus* Guam, Puerto Rico and the Virgin Islands.

9. *Q.* What is the difference between "residence" and "physical presence"?
    A. "Residence" as used in the naturalization law means "legal residence." It is the place to which a person, although temporarily absent, intends to return; the place at which a person votes. The law recognizes that people may be away from their "residence" for long periods of time. For example, American soldiers stationed overseas nevertheless retain their United States "residence." Similarly, many Americans are employed by companies in various foreign countries. These people retain their United States "residence."

    "Physical presence" means actual presence at a particular place. Thus, to satisfy the "physical presence" requirement of the law, the applicant must show that he was actually and bodily within the United States for the period of time required.

10. *Q.* How soon may a person vote after he has been naturalized?
    A. A person becomes a United States citizen immediately upon taking the oath of allegiance. Rules for voting, however, are established by the individual states. If the new citizen can meet the voting requirements, he may immediately register and vote in the next election.

    The Naturalization Law provides, however, that if the hearing on a petition is held less than sixty days before a general election, the applicant, although qualified for citizenship, will not be allowed to take the oath until ten days after the election. In this special case then, the new citizen could not vote until the next election.

11. *Q.* What happens if the applicant fails to pass his examination?
    A. Usually he is given further time for preparation and study and will be called again for examination at a later time.

12. *Q.* How may an adopted minor child who is not a citizen become a citizen of the United States?

   A. The child must be under eighteen years of age when a petition is filed on his behalf; he must have been lawfully admitted for permanent residence; he must have been adopted by United States citizens before his sixteenth birthday (under the law the adoption may occur either within or without the United States); he must have been legally in the custody of the adopted parents and a continuous resident of the United States for at least two years prior to the filing of the petition. Physical presence for one-half of this time is required.

13. *Q.* Why should every resident of the United States understand our country's government and history?

   A. The well-informed citizen is usually happier, better adjusted, more prosperous, and is much more valuable to his community, state and nation.

PATRIOTIC SONGS AND WRITINGS

STAR-SPANGLED BANNER

Oh, say! Can you see, by the dawn's early light,
What so proudly we hailed, at the twilight's last gleaming?
Whose broad stripes and bright stars, through the perilous fight,
O'er the ramparts we watched were so gallantly streaming.
And the rockets' red glare, the bombs bursting in air,
Gave proof through the night, that our flag was still there.

Chorus

Oh, say does the Star-Spangled Banner yet wave
O'er the land of the free and the home of the brave?

AMERICA

My country, 'tis of thee.
Sweet land of liberty.
 Of thee I sing;
Land where my fathers died!
Land of the Pilgrim's pride!
From every mountain-side
 Let freedom ring.

Our Fathers' God, to Thee,
Author of liberty,
 To Thee we sing;
Long may our land be bright
With freedom's holy light;
Protect us by Thy might,
 Great God, our King.

AMERICA, THE BEAUTIFUL

Oh, beautiful for spacious skies, for amber waves of grain,
For purple mountain majesties above the fruited plain!
America! America! God shed His grace on thee,
And crown thy good with brotherhood,
    From sea to shining sea!

Oh, beautiful for patriot dream that sees beyond the years,
Thine alabaster cities gleam undimmed by human tears!
America! America! God shed His grace on thee,
And crown thy good with brotherhood,
    From sea to shining sea!

THE DECLARATION OF INDEPENDENCE
IN CONGRESS, JULY 4, 1776
THE UNANIMOUS DECLARATION OF THE THIRTEEN
UNITED STATES OF AMERICA

When in the course of human events, it becomes necessary for one people to dissolve the political bands which have connected them with another, and to assume among the powers of the earth, the separate and equal station to which the laws of Nature and of Nature's God entitle them, a decent respect to the opinions of mankind requires that they should declare the causes which impel them to the separation.

We hold these truths to be self-evident, that all men are created equal, that they are endowed by their Creator with certain unalienable rights, that among these are life, liberty and the pursuit of happiness. That to secure these rights, governments are instituted among men, deriving their just powers from the consent of the governed, — That whenever any form of government becomes destructive to these ends, it is the right of the people to alter or to abolish it, and to institute new government, laying its foundation on such principles and organizing its powers in such form, as to them shall seem most likely to affect their safety and happiness. Prudence, indeed, will dictate that governments long established should not be changed for light and transient causes; and accordingly all experience hath shown, that mankind are more disposed to suffer, while evils are sufferable, than to right themselves by abolishing the forms to which they are accustomed. But when a long train of abuses and usurpations, pursuing invariably the same object evinces a design to reduce them under absolute despotism, it is their right, it is their duty, to throw off such government, and to provide new guards for their future security. — Such has been the patient sufferance of these Colonies; and such is now the necessity which constrains them to alter their former systems of government. The history of the present King of Great Britain is a history of repeated injuries and usurpations, all having in direct object the establishment of an absolute tyranny over these States . . .

(Here the Declaration lists the specific complaints of the Colonies against the King of England and concludes as follows:)

WE, THEREFORE, the Representatives of the United States of America, in General Congress Assembled, appealing to the Supreme Judge of the words for the rectitude of our intentions, do, in the name, and by authority of the good people of these Colonies, solemnly publish and declare, That these United Colonies are, and of right ought to be FREE AND INDEPENDENT STATES; that they are absolved from all allegiance to the British Crown, and that all political connection between them and the State of Great Britain, is and ought to be totally dissolved, and that as free and independent States, they have full power to levy war, conclude peace, contract alliances, establish commerce, and to do all other acts and things which independent States may of right do. And for the support of this Declaration, with a firm reliance on the protection of Divine Providence, we mutually pledge to each other our lives, our fortunes and our sacred honor.

LESSON II

OUR COUNTRY

There are four important divisions of North America. Canada is in the north, the United States is in the center, and Mexico is in the south. Between Mexico and South America is Central America.

The United States reaches from the Atlantic Ocean on the east to the Pacific Ocean on the west. It is twenty-five hundred miles from the eastern coast of this country to the western coast. From the Great Lakes on the north to the Gulf of Mexico on the south it is thirteen hundred miles.

There are two great mountain systems, the Appalachian in the east and the Rocky in the west. Between them is the immense Mississippi Valley. Through this valley flows the Mississippi River, one of the largest rivers in the world.

In the upper part of the Mississippi Valley are the five Great Lakes: Lakes Superior, Michigan, Huron, Erie and Ontario. They are the largest fresh-water lakes in the world. They are drained through the St. Lawrence River into the Atlantic Ocean.

Nature has given our country many places of great beauty and interest. Among the best known of the natural wonders are: Niagara Falls, between Lake Erie and Lake Ontario; the Mammoth Cave, in Kentucky; Glacier National Park, in Montana; Yellowstone Park, in Wyoming; the Grand Canyon of the Colorado, in Arizona; Yosemite Valley, in California; and Rainier National Park, in Washington.

The United States has many kinds of climate. The Pacific coast states have a mild climate, with a great deal of rain in the winter; the Southern states have warm summers and mild winters; the North Atlantic states and most of the states of the Mississippi Valley have warm summers and cold winters.

Fruits, grain, and vegetables in great abundance are raised in the United States. In many parts of the country there are large forests from which valuable lumber is obtained. Rich mines of iron, coal, lead, copper, gold, and silver are found in certain regions. On the farms and ranches there are vast numbers of cattle, hogs, horses, and other domestic animals. Wild animals, valuable for their fur, are still found in many places. In the cities are factories, shops, shipyards, and mills, giving employment to millions of men and women.

The United States has a splendid transportation system. Railroad and airplane lines cross all parts of the country, and passenger and freight boats ply in the navigable waters.

We have an excellent form of government in the United States. There are no classes privileged by birth, such as are found in many other countries. All citizens of this country have equal legal rights. The people, themselves, do the governing. In many European countries the people lost this power during the World War II period.

It is the duty of every resident of the United States to learn the main facts in regard to the history and government of our country. One who understands the government under which he lives can vote more intelligently and is more valuable to our country.

If an eligible foreign-born resident of the United States intends to remain here permanently, there are many reasons why he should become an American citizen. One who has his home in the United States and earns his living here can be of more value to the country if he becomes a citizen. He can vote for the right people to fill public offices and make our laws; he can sign petitions; he can serve on juries; he can hold office, and he can be of service in many other ways. If he has children, it is his duty to become a citizen.

The United States guarantees the protection of our government to all American citizens who may be unjustly treated in any foreign country.

Therefore, every qualified foreign-born resident of the United States owes it to himself, to his family, and to the country of his adoption, to be naturalized as soon as possible.

Every native-born American should be familiar with the essentials of our government in order that he may be an intelligent citizen and voter.

QUESTIONS AND ANSWERS

1. *Q.* What are the important divisions of North America?
   A. The important divisions of North America are Canada, the United States, Mexico and Central America.

2. *Q.* What is the extent of the United States?
   A. The United States measures twenty-five hundred miles from the Atlantic to the Pacific coast, and thirteen hundred miles from the northern to the southern boundary.

3. *Q.* What is the largest river in the United States?
   A. The Mississippi is the largest river.

4. *Q.* What are the two chief mountain systems?
   A. The two great mountain systems are the Rocky and the Appalachian.

5. Q. Name the Great Lakes.
   A. The Great Lakes are Lakes Superior, Michigan, Huron, Erie, and Ontario.

6. Q. What are some of the natural wonders of our country?
   A. Among the most noted are the Mammoth Cave, Niagara Falls, Glacier Park, Yellowstone Park, the Grand Canyon, Yosemite Valley, and the Rainier National Park.

7. Q. What are some of the important advantages of the United States?
   A. The United States has a great variety and abundance of vegetable and mineral products, excellent transportation systems, satisfactory climate, and one of the best organized governments in existence.

LESSON III

EARLY HISTORY

A few hundred years ago there were no white people in this country. The only inhabitants of the United States were copper-skinned people who had migrated originally from Asia and were called Indians by the first Europeans to arrive here. These Indians generally lived in small bands. They sustained themselves by hunting, fishing, and harvesting native plants. In some parts of the country these Indians were quarrelsome and roamed the countryside fighting other tribes and the white invaders. In other parts the tribes were peaceful, had settled homes, and primitive agricultural methods. They lived with the land and did not exhaust its resources.

We do not know for certain when the first white people came to America. There seems reason to believe that Norsemen, from Northern Europe, landed on the North Atlantic coast about the year 1000. If this be true, the expedition was of little value, as no permanent settlement was made. If any of the Norsemen remained in this country, they died of hardships, or were killed by the Indians, or intermarried with the Indians.

The real discovery of America in 1492 is attributed to Christopher Columbus. Columbus believed the earth to be round and the king and queen of Spain sent him, with three small ships, to try to find a short way to India by sailing west. He discovered San Salvador, a small island in the Atlantic, near the southeastern coast of the United States. He took possession in the name of Spain. Columbus made three more voyages to America.

Many other expeditions were fitted out to sail to the New World. Among the noted explorers was an Italian named Amerigo Vespucci. He made several voyages. Being interested in geography, he made several maps and wrote many letters describing his explorations. The result was that his name became prominently connected with the New World. Some years afterward, when Columbus and Vespucci were both dead, a book was written referring to the New World as "America." The name soon came into general use. It would have been more fitting, perhaps, for this land of ours to have been called "Columbia."

Spain, France, England, and Holland were the chief countries to send colonists to America. Sweden, also, sent explorers and colonists who settled about Delaware Bay.

The first permanent settlement in the United States was made by the Spaniards, at St. Augustine, Florida, in 1565. The second permanent settlement was also made by the Spaniards. This was at Santa Fe, New Mexico, in 1605.

Many of the Spanish explorers went into Mexico, Central America, and South America and made settlements. The Spanish language is still the chief language in those countries.

The first permanent English settlement was made at Jamestown, Virginia, in 1607. The colonists suffered great hardships at first. When they finally gave up the search for gold and silver and settled down to cultivate the rich soil they became more prosperous. The farmers in Virginia found it difficult to get enough laborers for their plantations. In 1619 Dutch slave traders brought a shipload of Negroes from Africa and sold them to the planters. This was the beginning of slavery, the great blot on our history for more than two hundred years.

In 1620 a band of English people known as the Pilgrims started for America, looking for a place where they might worship God as they pleased. After a stormy voyage in their small vessel, the Mayflower, they landed at Plymouth Rock, Massachusetts. There they made a settlement, the beginning of the New England States.

Many other English settlers followed the Pilgrims. They came for many reasons, the chief one being the desire for religious freedom. In twenty years there were more than twenty thousand white people in Massachusetts alone.

In 1609 the Dutch made a settlement at New Amsterdam. This was the beginning of the prosperous colony of New Netherlands. After some years the English took possession of the colony and changed the name to New York.

French fur traders and missionaries began to explore Canada at an early date. Their first settlements were made along the St. Lawrence River. They also settled in the Mississippi Valley and near the Great Lakes. The French have received credit for their successful efforts to bring Christianity to the Indians. Among the noted names of early French explorers are: Champlain, Marquette, Joliet, and LaSalle.

The early settlers endured many hardships while making homes in the New World. The forests had to be cut down and land prepared for the raising of crops. Supplies of all kinds had to be brought from Europe and were difficult to obtain. There were frequent fights with the Indians, who objected to the white people settling here.

The colonists were fortunate in having many brave and capable leaders who encouraged them to persevere and who managed their affairs wisely. Among the most noted of these leaders were Miles Standish of Plymouth,

John Smith of Virginia, Roger Williams of Rhode Island, William Penn of Pennsylvania, and Lord Baltimore in Maryland.

While America was being settled, England and France were constantly at war in Europe. It was natural that this war should spread to the New World. The English colonies and the French colonies engaged in four separate wars. They were: King William's War, 1689-1697; Queen Anne's War, 1702-1713; King George's War, 1743-1748, French and Indian War, 1754-1763.

In these wars some of the Indian tribes aided the French and some aided the English. In the last of these wars, which ended in 1763, England won a complete victory and was left in control of most of the country east of the Mississippi, including the colonies on the Atlantic coast. England also acquired Canada, which is still a part of the British Commonwealth. The year before the war closed France ceded her territory west of the Mississippi River to Spain but in 1800 it was secretly returned to France. The United States bought this territory from France in 1803. Florida remained a Spanish possession until 1819.

QUESTIONS

1. Q. What was the population of the United States at the time of the 1980 Federal census?
   A. Population in the United States in the 1980 census was estimated at 226,504,825.
2. Q. Who were the first inhabitants of the United States?
   A. The Indians were the first people who lived in the United States.
3. Q. When did the first white people come to America?
   A. It is believed that Norsemen, from Northern Europe, landed on the coast of America about the year 1000.
4. Q. Did the Norsemen make any permanent settlements?
   A. No, if any of them remained in America, they died of hardships or were killed by the Indians.
5. Q. When and by whom was the real discovery of America?
   A. Christopher Columbus, an Italian in the employ of Spain, discovered America in 1492.
6. Q. How did America receive its name?
   A. America was named for Amerigo Vespucci, a noted explorer, who made maps and wrote articles describing the new country.
7. Q. Did Spain send settlers to America?
   A. Yes, many people came from Spain. The Spaniards made the first permanent settlements in America.

8. *Q.* What were the first permanent settlements?
   A. The Spaniards founded St. Augustine, Florida, in 1565, and Santa Fe, New Mexico, in 1605.
9. *Q.* What other nations made settlements in America?
   A. England, France, and Holland were the most important nations to make settlements. A number of immigrants came from Sweden, also.
10. *Q.* Where were the first English settlements?
    A. The English settled Jamestown, Virginia, in 1607, and Plymouth, Massachusetts, in 1620.
11. *Q.* Why did the English come to America?
    A. Most of them came in order to secure freedom, especially freedom of religion. Some came to seek wealth and adventure.
12. *Q.* Where did the Dutch settle?
    A. The Dutch settled New Amsterdam (now New York) in 1609.
13. *Q.* Where were the first French settlements?
    A. The French settled along the St. Lawrence River in Canada, near the Great Lakes, and in the Mississippi Valley.
14. *Q.* How many wars were fought between the English and the French in America?
    A. There were four wars between the French and the English. The last of these, the "French and Indian War," ended in 1763.
15. *Q.* What was the final result of these wars?
    A. The English won a complete victory and secured control of the area now included in the eastern part of the United States. England also acquired Canada, which is still a part of the British Commonwealth.
16. *Q.* When was slavery introduced into the United States?
    A. Dutch slave traders, in 1619, brought a shipload of Africans to Virginia and sold them to the Jamestown planters. The importation of Negroes ceased in 1808, but slavery continued until 1865.
17. *Q.* Was slavery practiced in all parts of the United States?
    A. No, the practice of slavery was confined to the Southern States, where large plantations were common.
18. *Q.* When was slavery abolished?
    A. President Abraham Lincoln issued the "Emancipation Proclamation" in 1863, but the Confederate states continued the practice of slavery until the close of the Civil War in 1865.

SUMMARY OF DATES

1000 — Norsemen discovered northern America.
1492 — Columbus discovered America, took possession for Spain.

22

1565 — Spanish founded St. Augustine, Florida.
1605 — Spanish founded Santa Fe, New Mexico.
1607 — English founded Jamestown, Virginia.
1609 — Dutch (Hollanders) founded New Amsterdam (New York).
1619 — Slavery was introduced into Virginia.
1620 — English Pilgrims founded Plymouth, Massachusetts.
1620 - 1720 — People from many nations emigrated from Europe to America.
1763 — Last of four wars between English and French in America ended in a British victory. Thirteen British colonies were established.
1863 — President Abraham Lincoln issued the EMANCIPATION PROCLAMATION, abolishing slavery in the United States.
1865 — The Civil War ended. The nation was preserved and the slaves were freed.

LESSON IV

THE REVOLUTIONARY WAR

In 1760 there were thirteen well-established English colonies in America. These colonies were: Massachusetts, Rhode Island, Connecticut, New Hampshire, New York, New Jersey, Pennsylvania, Delaware, Virginia, Maryland, North Carolina, South Carolina, and Georgia.

The people of these colonies were industrious and ambitious. They had come to the New World for greater freedom and better living conditions.

They felt that they were entitled to make the most of new opportunities.

But they soon found that the English government did not intend to allow them the privileges for which they had hoped. The war between England and France had cost the English vast sums of money. In order to raise this money, England laid very heavy taxes on the colonists. The colonies were forbidden to trade with any country but England, and they had to send their products in English ships. The affairs of the colonies were regulated by English laws, many of which were distasteful to the people for whom they were intended. The colonies were not allowed to send representatives to the English Parliament to help make the laws, and they thought this to be very unfair.

Many of the leading men of the colonies advised that the people should not pay the English taxes unless they were allowed to send representatives to Parliament. "No taxation without representation" became the cry in all parts of the country.

In order to compel the Americans to pay the taxes and obey the laws, the English sent large numbers of soldiers to the colonies. The colonists were required to feed these soldiers and give them quarters. Instead of helping matters, this made them worse. There was constant trouble between the soldiers and the colonists. In 1770 a regiment of British soldiers in Boston fired into a crowd of men and boys who had annoyed them and wounded eleven. During the next few years there were several conflicts. Some of the leading men of the colonies, among them being Patrick Henry and Thomas Jefferson, advised fighting the English officers and soldiers until England would be compelled to give the colonies representation. In 1775 a Congress of delegates from the colonies met at Philadelphia and decided to fight the British until England gave them the right of self-government. George Washington was chosen to command the American army.

A volunteer army of Americans was immediately formed. After a year of fighting, which included the important battle of Bunker Hill, near Boston, the colonists decided that representation in Parliament was not enough, but that a new nation, entirely free from England, should be established.

On the Fourth of July, 1776, Congress issued the great "Declaration of Independence," which stated that the colonies were no longer under British rule, but were a free and independent nation. The Declaration of Independence gave a long list of reasons for the separation. Thomas Jefferson, one of America's most famous statesmen, was the chairman of a committee of five prominent men who wrote the Declaration of Independence.

After the Declaration of Independence was issued, the war between the two countries was known as the Revolutionary War. The war continued for six years. In 1778, through the influence of Benjamin Franklin, France sent ships and soldiers to help the Americans. The French army gave valuable aid to the American troops during the next three years. Marquis de Lafayette, a young nobleman, was one of the Frenchmen who served with distinction in the American army.

Among other distinguished Europeans who rendered valuable service in the American forces were Thaddeus Kosciuszko and Casimir Pulaski, from Poland; Baron Friedrich Wilhelm von Steuben, a trained German officer; and Count D'Estaing, a French naval officer.

The last engagement of the war was in 1781, when Lord Cornwallis, the British commander, surrendered at Yorktown, Virginia, to George Washington. Shortly afterward, all British armies were withdrawn from the United States. A treaty of peace was signed in 1783, and our country began her existence as a free nation.

QUESTIONS

1. *Q.* How many British colonies were there in America in 1760?
   A. There were thirteen British colonies.
2. *Q.* Why did these colonies become dissatisfied with British rule?
   A. The colonies objected to "taxation without representation." England imposed very high taxes upon the colonists and did not allow them to send representatives to Parliament to help make the laws. England appointed officers for the colonies and sent over soldiers to enforce the laws. The colonies had to support these soldiers. All exports from the colonies had to be sent in English ships.
3. *Q.* When did actual trouble between the colonies and England begin?
   A. There was considerable difficulty between 1770 and 1775. In 1775 war really began, with George Washington as Commander-in-chief of the American army.
4. *Q.* For what were the colonies fighting at first?
   A. They were fighting at first for representative government.
5. *Q.* When was the Declaration of Independence issued?
   A. The Declaration of Independence was published July 4, 1776.
6. *Q.* Who issued the Declaration of Independence?
   A. The Continental Congress, meeting at Philadelphia. Thomas Jefferson, one of our great statesmen, wrote the Declaration of Independence.
7. *Q.* What did the Declaration of Independence declare?
   A. It declared that the colonies "are and ought to be, a free and independent nation." It gave a long list of reasons for separation from England.
8. *Q.* What country aided the United States in the Revolutionary War?
   A. France gave valuable aid. Many individuals from other countries volunteered important service.
9. *Q.* When did the Revolutionary War end?
   A. Lord Cornwallis, the British general, surrendered to Washington at Yorktown, Virginia in 1781. The peace treaty was signed in 1783.

LESSON V

OUR FLAG

"There are many flags in many lands,
There are flags of every hue,
But there is no flag, however grand,
Like our own red, white and blue."

The United States flag is often called the "Stars and Stripes," or the "Red, White and Blue," or "Old Glory." Our country has had this flag as her emblem since 1777. The honor of making the first flag is credited to Betsy Ross, a patriotic woman of Philadelphia. It is said that George Washington made a pencil sketch of the design — thirteen stripes of alternate red and white, and thirteen white stars in a circle on a blue background. This sketch was submitted to Betsy Ross. Our beautiful flag is the result of her work.

On the first flag each of the original thirteen states was represented by a stripe and a star. As new states were added to the Union, new stars were added. The number of stripes varied, but was finally fixed permanently at thirteen. Our flag now has fifty stars, each representing one of the fifty states, and thirteen stripes, each standing for one of the thirteen states which won their independence through the Revolutionary War. The stars are white on a field of blue and are arranged in nine staggered rows. Five of the rows have six stars and the remaining rows have five stars. The fifty states represented by stars on the flag, arranged in the order in which they entered the Union under the present Constitution are:

Delaware, Pennsylvania, New Jersey, Georgia, Connecticut, Massachusetts, Maryland, South Carolina, New Hampshire, Virginia, New York, North Carolina, Rhode Island, Vermont, Kentucky, Tennessee, Ohio, Louisiana, Indiana, Mississippi, Illinois, Alabama, Maine, Missouri, Arkansas, Michigan, Florida, Texas, Iowa, Wisconsin, California, Minnesota, Oregon, Kansas, West Virginia, Nevada, Nebraska, Colorado, North Dakota, South Dakota, Montana, Washington, Idaho, Wyoming, Utah, Oklahoma, New Mexico, Arizona, Alaska and Hawaii.

Each color in the flag has a meaning. The red stands for courage, the white stands for truth, the blue stands for justice. That we may have constantly in mind these American ideals, our flag floats over every public building and is found in every school-room.

The flag should be raised at sunrise and lowered at sunset.

The American flag should always have the place of honor when carried with other flags.

The flag should not be used in any form of advertising.

When the flag becomes soiled or worn it should be respectfully burned.

A special day, June 14th, has been designated "Flag Day." On this day the flag is publicly honored by patriotic exercises, and Americans renew their pledge of loyalty. Every American should know this pledge of allegiance:

"I pledge allegiance to the flag of the United States of America, and to the republic for which it stands; one nation under God, indivisible, with liberty and justice for all."

QUESTIONS

1. *Q.* What are the colors of the United States flag?
   A. The colors of the flag are red, white and blue.
2. *Q.* For what do these colors stand?
   A. Red stands for courage, white stands for truth, and blue stands for justice.
3. *Q.* How many stripes are there on the flag?
   A. There are thirteen stripes. Each represents one of the original thirteen states.
4. *Q.* What are the original thirteen states?
   A. They are Massachusetts, Rhode Island, Connecticut, New Hampshire, New York, New Jersey, Pennsylvania, Delaware, Virginia, Maryland, North Carolina, South Carolina, Georgia.
5. *Q.* How many stars are there on the flag?
   A. There are fifty stars. Each represents one of the present fifty states.
6. *Q.* Repeat the pledge of allegiance.
   A. "I pledge allegiance to the flag of the United States of America, and to the republic for which it stands; one nation under God, indivisible, with liberty and justice for all."

LESSON VI

HOW THE CONSTITUTION WAS MADE

After the Declaration of Independence was issued on July 4th, 1776, a Congress, composed of delegates from the thirteen colonies formulated a plan of government for the new nation. The government was to be a republic. This system of laws was called the "Articles of Confederation."

It was soon found that the "Articles" were not satisfactory. There was no president or executive head. Congress could make laws but could not enforce them. Any state could withdraw from the union if it wished to do so.

After a few years, the people decided that the Articles of Confederation must be improved. In 1787, delegates from the thirteen states met at Philadelphia to make a new Constitution. Their intention at that time was to revise and improve the Articles of Confederation. It was soon evident, however, that alteration of the Articles of Confederation would not be sufficient for the needs of the rapidly growing nation, and that an entirely new constitution must be made.

The Convention of 1787 at Philadelphia drafted the present Constitution, which provided that it was to become binding as soon as nine states had ratified it.

The new Constitution was a great improvement over the Articles of Confederation. Indeed, it is so excellent that, although over 200 years have passed since its adoption, there have been but 26 changes or amendments to the original Constitution.

Many of the ablest men of the new nation were members of the convention. Among them were George Washington, Alexander Hamilton, James Madison, Benjamin Franklin, Elbridge Gerry, and Robert Morris.

The convention began its sessions in May and it was not until September that the Constitution was ready to be submitted to the several states.

Some of the states represented were large and some were small; some were agricultural and some largely commercial; some were slave states and some free. Many heated debates and discussions took place among the delegates before acceptable compromises were finally reached.

Under the Articles of Confederation there was but one house of Congress. Each state had one vote, regardless of the number of delegates. This was distasteful to large states like Virginia and Massachusetts, which had no more power in Congress than the small state of Delaware. The new Constitution compromised this situation satisfactorily by establishing two houses in Congress. In the Senate all states were to have equal representation; in the House of Representatives the representation was to depend upon population. In both houses every member was to have an independent vote.

The slavery compromises included the counting of three-fifths of all slaves in determining representation, and the forbidding of slave-importation after 1808.

Other compromises included the election of United States Senators by the state legislatures, the election of the President by Presidential electors, and the appointment of the Supreme Court Justices by the President, with the consent of the Senate.

The adoption of the new Constitution was vigorously opposed in several of the states, but enough had accepted it by the summer of 1788 to put it into effect. Rhode Island and North Carolina held out until the last. The government went into operation with the inauguration of Washington as President in New York City, April 30, 1789.

QUESTIONS

1. *Q.* What form of government has the United States?
   A. The United States is a republic. We have a republican form of government.
2. *Q.* What is a republic?
   A. A republic is a government by the people through their elected representatives. The highest officer is a President, elected by the people.
3. *Q.* What is the constitution?
   A. The Constitution is the supreme law of the United States.
4. *Q.* Upon what principles is the United States Constitution based?
   A. The principles of the Constitution are Liberty, Equality, and Justice.
5. *Q.* What was the first system of laws of the United States called?
   A. It was called the "Articles of Confederation." This was adopted during the Revolutionary War.
6. *Q.* Why were the Articles of Confederation unsatisfactory?
   A. Under the Articles of Confederation there was no President. Congress could make laws but could not enforce them. Any state could withdraw from the Union if it chose.
7. *Q.* When was the present Constitution written?
   A. Delegates from the thirteen states met at Philadelphia and made a new constitution in 1787.
8. *Q.* How many states were required to ratify the Constitution?
   A. When nine states had ratified the Constitution it was to be binding among those states.
9. *Q.* When was the Constitution ratified?
   A. It was ratified by nine states in 1788, and was adopted in 1789. It had been ratified by all states in 1790.

LESSON VII

THE CONSTITUTION AND THE PRESIDENT

The United States Constitution which was adopted in 1789 created the office of President. A President was to be elected every four years and was to serve as many terms as the people wished. George Washington was the unanimous choice for first President. He became President in 1789 and served two terms. He declined a third term. Several of our Presidents have served two terms, but no one was elected to a third term except Franklin D. Roosevelt. A recent amendment to the constitution, the 22nd, limits the number of terms to *two*.

On November 22, 1963, the world was shocked by the assassination of President Jchn F. Kennedy in Dallas, Texas. Vice-President Lyndon B. Johnson immediately succeeded to the presidency and served out the remaining term. He was reelected for a four year term in November 1964.

Our fifth President, James Monroe, in a message to Congress in 1823, announced it as his opinion that no foreign countries should thereafter attempt to colonize any part of the American continent, and said that any attempt to do so would be regarded by the United States as an "unfriendly act." This has since been known as the "Monroe Doctrine," and the principle has been generally agreed upon internationally.

Four of our Presidents, Lincoln, Garfield, McKinley and Kennedy, met death at the hands of assassins. Two others, William Henry Harrison and Zachary Taylor, died shortly after inauguration.

Woodrow Wilson, after many months of failing health, died in January, 1924. Mr. Wilson carried the heavy burdens of the Presidency during World War I and his unselfish devotion to his duties undermined his health. He will be remembered as one of our greatest Presidents.

On April 12, 1945, less than six weeks before the surrender of Germany in World War II, President Franklin D. Roosevelt died. Vice-President Harry S. Truman at once assumed the office of President.

The people of the United States have usually displayed great wisdom in the choice of their Chief Executives. Most of the Presidents have been men of ability, who have served their country well in the high office to which they have been elected.

LIST OF PRESIDENTS

1. George Washington 1789-1797
2. John Adams 1797-1801

3. Thomas Jefferson 1801-1809
4. James Madison 1809-1817
5. James Monroe 1817-1825
6. John Quincy Adams 1825-1829
7. Andrew Jackson 1829-1837
8. Martin Van Buren 1837-1841
9. William Henry Harrison . . . 1841-
10. John Tyler 1841-1845
11. James K. Polk 1845-1849
12. Zachary Taylor 1849-1850
13. Millard Fillmore 1850-1853
14. Franklin Pierce 1853-1857
15. James Buchanan 1857-1861
16. Abraham Lincoln 1861-1865
17. Andrew Johnson 1865-1869
18. Ulysses S. Grant 1869-1877
19. Rutherford B. Hayes 1877-1881
20. James A. Garfield 1881-
21. Chester A. Arthur 1881-1885
22. Grover Cleveland 1885-1889
23. Benjamin Harrison 1889-1893
24. Grover Cleveland 1893-1897
25. William McKinley 1897-1901
26. Theodore Roosevelt 1901-1909
27. William H. Taft 1909-1913
28. Woodrow Wilson 1913-1921
29. Warren G. Harding 1921-1923
30. Calvin Coolidge 1923-1929
31. Herbert Hoover 1929-1933
32. Franklin D. Roosevelt 1933-1945
33. Harry S. Truman 1945-1953
34. Dwight D. Eisenhower 1953-1961
35. John F. Kennedy 1961-1963
36. Lyndon B. Johnson 1963-1969
37. Richard M. Nixon 1969-1974
38. Gerald R. Ford 1974-1977
39. Jimmy Carter 1977-1981
40. Ronald Reagan 1981-1989
41. George Bush 1989-

QUESTIONS AND ANSWERS

1. *Q.* Who was the first President of the United States?
   A. George Washington became President of the United States in 1789.

2. *Q.* How many Presidents have we had in the United States?
   A. Forty men have served as President. Grover Cleveland served twice.

3. *Q.* Who was President during the Civil War?
   A. Abraham Lincoln was President at that time.

4. *Q.* How many terms may a President serve?
   A. Until the adoption of Amendment 22, in March 1951, a President could serve as many terms as he might be elected. Franklin D. Roosevelt was elected for four successive terms.

   Amendment 22 limits to *two* the number of terms to which a President may be elected.

5. *Q.* What Presidents were assassinated in office? ·
   A. Abraham Lincoln, James Garfield, William McKinley and John F. Kennedy met death at the hands of assassins.

6. *Q.* How often is a President elected?
   A. Presidential elections are held every four years. Electors are chosen in November of the years divisible by four. They elect the President in the December following.

7. *Q.* When does the President take office?
   A. The President takes office on the twentieth of January following his election.

8. *Q.* What is the Monroe Doctrine?
   A. The Monroe Doctrine declares that no foreign power shall ever, hereafter, make attempts to colonize any part of America. It was announced in 1823. It has been invoked successfully on several occasions when foreign nations suggested colonization of some part of America.

9. *Q.* Who called a republic "a government of the people, by the people and for the people"?
   A. Abraham Lincoln used these words in his famous "Gettysburg Address." This address was given in November, 1863, at the dedication of a portion of the Gettysburg battlefield as a National Cemetery.

   (For text of Gettysburg Address see page 2.)

LESSON VIII

LEGISLATIVE BRANCH OF THE NATIONAL GOVERNMENT

The supreme law of the United States is the Constitution. The Constitution divides the government of the nation into three branches called the legislative branch, the executive branch and the judicial branch. Legislative means law making; executive means law enforcing; judicial means law interpreting. We have these three branches in the government of the nation, the government of the state, the government of the county and the government of the city. If a citizen understands the working of these three branches, he will have good knowledge of the government of our nation.

The legislative branch of the United States is Congress. Congress meets in Washington, D.C. on the 3rd day of January of each year. It usually remains in session until its business for the year is completed. The President may call a special session when he thinks it necessary. Several Presidents have called special sessions of Congress.

Congress is made up of two houses. One house is called the Senate, and the other is called the House of Representatives. Each of the fifty states in the Union sends two Senators to the United States Senate, this makes a total of 100 United States Senators. The term of office is six years. One-third of the Senators go out of office every two years. Senators represent their states as a whole. A Senator may reside in any part of the State which he represents.

The number of Representatives from any state depends upon the population of the state. Each state is entitled to at least one Representative, no matter how small its population. The basis of representation is changed every ten years, following the taking of the United States census. When the Constitution was adopted the basis was one Representative for every 30,000 people. At present the basis is one Representative for every 410,481 people.

Representatives are usually called Congressmen. Each state is divided into Congressional districts. It is customary for a Representative to be a resident of the district which he represents. A Representative serves two years.

The present House of Representatives has 435 members plus a Resident Commissioner from Puerto Rico. The latter has no vote but does take part in discussions and may request the House to consider problems which are of interest to his home area.

A U. S. Senator must be at least thirty years old. A Representative must be at least twenty-five years old.

The Vice-President of the United States presides over the Senate and is called the President of the Senate. He is elected at the same time and in the

33

same manner as is the President of the United States. When the Vice-President is called upon to act as President of the United States or is absent for any other reason, the President *pro tempore* of the Senate presides over the Senate. Dan Quayle is the current Vice-President.

The Vice-President can vote only in case of a tie in the Senate. For example, if fifty Senators voted for a bill and fifty voted against it, the Vice-President might cast the deciding vote. But the President pro tempore, being a member of the Senate, may vote on all questions, whether he is presiding or not. When the Vice-President votes on a tie it is always to pass the measure. He does not vote against a measure. If it is a tie and he does not vote, the measure is lost, automatically.

The presiding officer of the House of Representatives is called the Speaker. The Speaker is one of the members of the House of Representatives, and is elected by his fellow members. As the Speaker is one of the Representatives, he can vote on all questions. He will succeed to the office of President of the United States if both President and Vice-President are unable to serve. A Speaker pro tempore is chosen by the Representatives, to preside when the Speaker is absent.

MEMBERSHIP IN HOUSE OF REPRESENTATIVES

Alabama 7, Alaska 1, Arizona 5, Arkansas 4, California 45, Colorado 6, Connecticut 6, Delaware 1, Florida 19, Georgia 10, Hawaii 2, Idaho 2, Illinois 22, Indiana 19, Iowa 6, Kansas 5, Kentucky 7, Louisiana 8, Maine 2, Maryland 8, Massachusetts 11, Michigan 18, Minnesota 8, Mississippi 5, Missouri 9, Montana 2, Nebraska 3, Nevada 2, New Hampshire 2, New Jersey 14, New Mexico 3, New York 34, North Carolina 11, North Dakota 1, Ohio 23, Oklahoma 6, Oregon 5, Pennsylvania 23, Rhode Island 2, South Carolina 6, South Dakota 1, Tennessee 9, Texas 27, Utah 3, Vermont 1, Virginia 10, Washington 8, West Virginia 4, Wisconsin 9, Wyoming 1 — Total 435.

QUESTIONS

1. *Q.* What are the three branches of government in the United States?
   A. The three branches are the legislative, the executive, and the judicial.

2. *Q.* What is the meaning of these three terms?
   A. Legislative means law-making; executive means law-enforcing; judicial means law-interpreting or law-explaining.

3. *Q.* What is the legislative branch of the United States government?
   A. Congress is the legislative branch of the United States government.

4. Q. Where and when does Congress meet?
   A. Congress meets in Washington, D.C., on the third day of January, each year. It continues in session most of the year.

5. Q. What are the divisions of Congress?
   A. Congress is made up of two houses, the House of Representatives and the Senate.

6. Q. How many United States Senators does each state have?
   A. Each state has two United States Senators.

7. Q. How many Representatives does a state have?
   A. The number of Representatives depends upon the population of the state. In the present Congress the Representatives are allocated among the states on the basis of the total population which was established by the 1980 Census; there is one Representative for each 410,481 persons.

8. Q. Who presides over the Senate?
   A. The Vice-President is President of the Senate.

9. Q. Who presides over the House of Representatives?
   A. The presiding officer is the Speaker, who is elected by his fellow members. A law passed by Congress in 1947 made the Speaker the successor to the Presidency of the United States if both President and Vice-President are unable to serve.

10. Q. Are the duties of U.S. Senators and Representatives the same?
    A. A U.S. Senator is expected to look after the interests of his entire state. A Representative's first duty is to promote the interests of the district which elects him. Both are expected to work for the good of all the people.

11. Q. Did the number of members in the House of Representatives increase as a result of the 1980 Census returns?
    A. No, the permanent number continued at 435. A new basis was established as a result of the 1980 Census and the division of Representatives among the states was adjusted on that basis. Some states gained Representatives, others lost.

       Gains in representation: California 2, Florida 4, Texas 3, Arizona, Colorado, Washington, Tennessee, Oregon, Nevada, Utah, New Mexico, 1 each.

       Losses in representation: New York 5, Pennsylvania, Ohio, Illinois 2 each, Indiana, Massachusetts, Michigan, Missouri, New Jersey and South Dakota 1 each.

12. *Q.* Why is the present Congress called the 102nd Congress?

    A. Since the United States Constitution was adopted in 1789, members of the House of Representatives have been elected 101 times for two-year terms.

    In the 102nd Congress the Democrats have a majority in the House and in the Senate.

13. *Q.* In a republic the people govern through their representatives. Why do not the voters govern directly, instead of electing representatives?

    A. In the early days of New England there were townships in which all the voters met for the purpose of making laws. There were few people in these townships, and they lived in a small area. This kind of direct government would not be possible under modern conditions. There are too many people in a voting district. Most of them could not leave their homes or their businesses; many would have too far to go; most of them could not spare the time; a great many would be unsuited for taking part, through lack of information and experience.

    In the representative plan voters may choose a small number of educated and experienced representatives who will more capably make laws and govern for them, usually carrying out their wishes as expressed. Many of the members of our present Congress are lawyers by profession.

LESSON IX

LAW-MAKING

All laws made in the United States must agree with the principles of the Constitution. Laws are made by both houses of Congress working together. Neither the Senate nor the House of Representatives can make laws alone.

A proposed law is called a bill. There are three ways in which bills may become laws.

First Way: A bill must pass both houses of Congress by a majority vote. It must then be sent to the President. If the President signs the bill it becomes a law.

Second Way: A bill must pass both houses by a majority vote and be sent to the President. If the President vetoes the bill, he sends it back to the house in which it started. If both houses pass it again by a two-thirds majority vote, it becomes a law without the President's signature.

Third Way: A bill must pass both houses by a majority vote and be sent to the President. If the President keeps it ten days (Sundays excepted), it becomes a law without his signature, unless Congress adjourns before the ten days are up.

Orders and resolutions which require the concurrence of both houses must also be sent to the President for his signature or veto.

Congress sometimes passes laws which are needed for a short time only, and sometimes passes laws which prove unsatisfactory. The Constitution provides that all laws passed by Congress may be repealed or changed by Congress.

POWERS OF CONGRESS

Congress gets its power from the people, who elect the members of Congress. The power of law-making is expressly given to Congress by the Constitution of the United States. Article X of the Bill of Rights says: "The powers not delegated to the United States by the constitution, nor prohibited by it to the states, are reserved to the states respectively, or to the people." With this restriction, Congress has power to make all laws necessary for the welfare of the nation. Only a few of the most important powers are mentioned in the constitution. Among them are the following:

(1) Congress can declare war. The President may recommend that war be declared, but Congress alone can declare war. (2) Congress makes laws for the naturalization of foreigners. These laws must be the same in all parts of the United States. (3) Congress can establish and partially control post offices.

(4) Congress can establish courts when necessary. (5) Congress can coin money. (6) Congress can grant patents and copyrights. (7) Congress can raise money for government expenses by taxing goods imported from other countries and certain goods manufactured at home. (8) Congress has some authority over the governing of the District of Columbia. This is a tract of land comprising about seventy square miles, set aside for the seat of the United States government. It is located between the States of Maryland and Virginia, and contains the city of Washington, the National capital.

The city of Washington does not control its own affairs as do other cities, because Congress has some authority over it.

PROHIBITIONS ON CONGRESS

A prohibition is something which is forbidden. The Constitution prohibits Congress from doing certain things.

1. Congress cannot tax goods exported from the United States. These goods will probably be taxed in the country to which they go. It would be unfair to tax them here, also.

2. Congress cannot grant titles of nobility. Our country is a democracy and we cannot have Counts, Dukes, Barons, or Lords among American citizens.

3. Congress cannot spend United States money except as prescribed by law.

4. Congress cannot stop the right of *habeas corpus* except in war time. The right of *habeas corpus* is one of the most valuable rights of a free people. It means that no one can be held in prison without a trial.

In time of war it is sometimes thought necessary to imprison people whose actions are suspicious. The right of *habeas corpus* may be suspended in such cases.

5. Congress cannot pass an *ex post facto* law. An *ex post facto* law is a law that changes the penalty after an offense has been committed, or makes punishable an offense which was not punishable when committed. An *ex post facto* law alters the situation of the accused person. No such law can ever be passed in the United States.

6. Congress cannot pass a bill of attainder, a measure which inflicts punishment without ordinary judicial trial. The bill of attainder was formerly in operation in some European countries. Under this law also, persons convicted of certain serious offenses were deprived of all civil rights. They could not inherit property or leave property to their children. Their blood was said to be "attainted," or stained by disgrace.

PROHIBITIONS ON THE STATES

Each of the fifty states in the Union has its own constitution and has a legislature to make laws for the people of that state. The United States Constitution has placed certain prohibitions on the states, mainly to prevent them from passing laws which are the business of the national government.

1. No state can declare war. Congress only can declare war. A state may, however, defend itself if invaded.
2. No state can coin money.
3. No state can make treaties with other states or with foreign countries.
4. No state can tax exported or imported goods.
5. No state can grant titles of nobility.

DIFFERING FUNCTIONS OF GOVERNMENT

The national government gives us military protection, personal freedom, uniform citizenship rights, and subsidizes the postal service. The state government gives us many state institutions, educational privileges, state highways, water rights, insurance regulations, railroad regulations, and protection of game. The county gives us tax regulations, institutions for the sick and dependent, and aid for widows and orphans. The city gives us police and fire protection, street improvements, and school facilities.

QUESTIONS

1. Q. With what must all laws in the United States agree?
   A. All laws must agree with the principles of the Constitution of the United States.
2. Q. What is the meaning of veto?
   A. Veto means to refuse assent, to prohibit.
3. Q. In how many ways do bills become laws?
   A. Bills become laws in three ways: by a majority vote of both houses of Congress and the signature of the President; by a two-thirds majority vote of both houses of Congress over the President's veto; by the President's keeping the bill ten days (Sundays excepted).
4. Q. May United States laws be changed?
   A. All laws passed by Congress may be changed or repealed by Congress.
5. Q. Where does Congress get its powers?
   A. The powers of Congress are given by the people through the Constitution of the United States.

6. *Q.* What are some of the important powers of Congress?
   A. Congress can declare war, establish and partially control post offices, establish courts, coin money, grant patents and copyrights, raise money for national expenses, and make laws for the naturalization of foreigners.
7. *Q.* What is the District of Columbia?
   A. The District of Columbia is a small tract of land set aside by Congress as the seat of government of the United States. It contains the city of Washington.
8. *Q.* What is a prohibition?
   A. A prohibition is the forbidding of something by law.
9. *Q.* What are some of the things which the Constitution prohibits Congress from doing?
   A. Congress cannot tax exports, suspend the right of *habeas corpus* except in war time, or pass an *ex post facto* law or a bill of attainder.
10. *Q.* What is a writ of *habeas corpus?*
    A. *Habeas corpus* is a guarantee of personal freedom. It means that no person can be held in jail without a trial.
11. *Q.* What is an *ex post facto* law?
    A. An *ex post facto* law is a law which changes the penalty for an offense after the offense has been committed. It is forbidden by the Constitution.
12. *Q.* What is a bill of attainder?
    A. A bill of attainder is a law which punishes people without ordinary judicial trial. Formerly, in some countries, the bill of attainder deprived certain convicted persons of civil rights, and prevented them from inheriting or transmitting property.
13. *Q.* What are some of the prohibitions on the states?
    A. States cannot declare war, coin money, grant titles of nobility, or make treaties.
14. *Q.* We have a Federal government to govern the entire United States. We have, also, fifty state governments. Why cannot Congress make all the laws, and do away with the state governments?
    A. Some laws and regulations must be the same in all states; postal regulations, money values, the number of years' residence required in order that an alien may become a citizen, Federal income tax laws, and many others which must apply to all people.

    There are other laws and regulations that are necessary or desirable in some states, but not in others. For example, sea-coast states need harbor laws that would be useless in inland states; states with mines and states with timber need laws that are not required in states that do not have these resources; the people of various states differ in their wishes in regard to laws regulating marriage and divorce. The authors of the Constitution of the United States wisely provided that these matters are left to the state governments, providing that all laws made agree with the principles of the Federal Constitution.

15. Q. What are some of the things done for us by the national government?
    A. The national government gives us naturalization laws, passports, military protection, personal freedom, and subsidizes the postal service.
16. Q. What does the state give us?
    A. The state gives us many state institutions, educational privileges, state highways, insurance and railroad regulations, and protection of game.
17. Q. What does the county give us?
    A. The county gives us institutions for the sick and dependent, aid for widows and orphans, and tax regulations.
18. Q. What does the city give us?
    A. The city give us police and fire protection, street improvements, parks, playgrounds, and educational facilities.

LESSON X

POWERS OF THE SENATE AND HOUSE OF REPRESENTATIVES SEPARATELY

All United States laws are made by the Senate and the House of Representatives working together. Each house has, in addition, certain powers which are not given to the other house.

THE SENATE

Many of the important officers are appointed by the President, only with the consent of the Senate. Among these officers are members of the Cabinet and judges of all United States courts.

Ambassadors and consuls to foreign countries are also appointed by the President with the consent of the Senate. Ambassadors represent our government in diplomatic relations with the governments of other important countries. Consuls protect American citizens and promote the interests of our trade in foreign countries. Many foreign countries send ambassadors to Washington. Foreign consuls are stationed in Seattle, San Francisco, Los Angeles, New York, and other important cities.

Among the countries which have consuls stationed in San Francisco and Los Angeles are Australia, Belgium, China, Denmark, Finland, Greece, Great Britain, Irish Republic, Israel, Japan, Korea, Mexico, Netherlands, Norway, Panama, Portugal, the Philippines, Spain, Sweden, Switzerland, France, and the countries of South America and Central America.

Treaties with foreign countries are made by the President with the consent of the Senate. After the close of World War I, President Wilson reccommended that the United States sign the international agreement known as the League of Nations, but the Senate refused its consent.

HOUSE OF REPRESENTATIVES

The House of Representatives has the power to originate all bills for raising revenue. As the Representatives represent the people directly, it is only fair that the power of originating tax-measures be given them. The Senate must vote on all bills for raising revenue, the same as on other bills.

The Constitution provides that certain Federal officers may be impeached. Among them are the President and Vice-President and Federal Judges. Impeachment means officially accusing an officer of wrong-doing. In the case of United States officers, the House of Representatives impeaches and the Senate tries the cases.

Andrew Johnson, who became President after Abraham Lincoln's death, was the only President of the United States ever impeached. President Johnson had trouble with Congress because he removed a Cabinet officer without the consent of the Senate. He was impeached and tried, but there was lacking one vote of the two-thirds necessary to convict him, and he was acquitted.

In 1974, President Nixon, besieged by a rising tide of demands for his impeachment, resigned. His vice-president, Gerald R. Ford, whom he appointed to take Spiro Agnew's place, became the 38th president.

Usually, the Vice-President of the United States presides over the Senate. If a President is being tried, however, the Vice-President does not preside, as he is very likely to be prejudiced. The Constitution provides that the Chief Justice of the United States shall preside during the trial of a President.

QUESTIONS

1. Q. What powers has the Senate which the House of Representatives has not?
   A. The President must have the consent of the Senate when he appoints Cabinet officers, judges of United States courts, and ambassadors and consuls to foreign countries; the President must have the consent of the Senate when he makes treaties; the Senate tries cases of impeachment, the Senate has the power to elect a Vice-President of the United States in case the Presidential electors fail to elect one.

2. Q. What powers has the House of Representatives?
   A. The House of Representatives originates all bills for raising revenue; it impeaches United States officers; the House of Representatives elects a President of the United States if the Presidential electors fail to elect one.

3. Q. What does impeachment mean?
   A. Impeachment means officially accusing an officer of wrong-doing.

4. Q. What President was impeached?
   A. Andrew Johnson, who became President after the death of Lincoln, was impeached. The Senate acquitted him by one vote. In 1974 President Nixon resigned to avoid putting the country through the impeachment process.

5. Q. What is the penalty if an impeached officer is found guilty?
   A. He is removed from office and can never hold office again. If he has committed a crime he may be tried in the regular courts.

6. Q. Who usually presides over the United States Senate?
   A. The Vice-President of the United States usually presides over the Senate.

7. Q. Who presides over the Senate when the Vice-President becomes President of the United States?
   A. The President *pro tempore* of the Senate presides until the approval of a new Vice-President.

8. Q. When the Vice-President succeeds to the Presidency, who takes the office of Vice-President?
   A. The person nominated by the President and confirmed by both Houses of Congress takes office.

9. Q. Who presides over the Senate when the President is tried?
   A. The Chief Justice of the United States Supreme Court presides, because the Vice-President may be prejudiced.

43

LESSON XI

EXECUTIVE BRANCH OF THE NATIONAL GOVERNMENT

The executive branch of government is the law-enforcing branch. The Chief Executive of the United States is the President. The President's term of office is four years. A President must be at least thirty-five years old when he is elected. No naturalized citizen can be President or Vice-President. The Constitution says that both of these officers must be native-born citizens. Naturalized citizens are eligible to all other offices in the United States.

If the President dies, resigns, or is unable, for any other reason, to continue in his office, the Vice-President becomes President. If both President and Vice-President are unable to serve as President, the Speaker of the House of Representatives succeeds to the office. Following the Speaker in the line of succession are the President *pro tem* of the Senate, the Secretary of State, the Secretary of the Treasury, and other Cabinet members in order. Should any member of the Cabinet be a naturalized citizen, he would not be eligible to the Presidency. The office would pass to the next in order. Henry Kissinger, Secretary of State under President Nixon, is a naturalized citizen. He was, therefore, not eligible for the office of President.

The President has many important powers and duties. Among them are the following: He sees that the laws are enforced; he signs or vetoes bills sent to him by Congress; he is Commander-in-Chief of the Army and Navy of the United States; he grants pardons, reprieves, and commutations for offenses against United States laws; he sends an annual message to Congress telling what he thinks are the needs of the country; he calls special sessions of Congress when necessary; he fills vacancies in certain offices; with the consent of the Senate he makes treaties and appoints ambassadors and consuls to foreign countries, members of the Cabinet, and judges of the United States courts.

The President is elected by the people, but not directly. The people cast their votes for Presidential electors, and these Presidential electors elect the President. The number of Presidential electors to which any state is entitled is equal to the number of Representatives from that state plus the number of United States Senators. In 1988, California had 43 Representatives and two U.S. Senators. Therefore, California was entitled to 45 Presidential electors. (The Presidential electors are not members of Congress. They are men and women elected solely as Presidential electors.)

The Presidential electors are elected on the first Tuesday after the first Monday in November, every fourth year. National conventions for the purpose of nominating candidates for President and Vice-President are held by political parties during the summer preceding the November election.

A person who wishes to vote for President casts his ballot for the electors who have been previously nominated by his political party. These electors are pledged to vote for the candidate who was nominated for the Presidency at the National Convention of their party some months before.

Since the Presidential electors are pledged to vote for their party candidate, it is known almost immediately after their election whether one of the candidates has a majority. But the actual election does not take place until the following month. On the Monday after the second Wednesday in December following the November election, the Presidential electors meet at the capitals of their respective states and cast their ballots for President and Vice-President. They make three lists of the votes cast. One list is sent to Congress by messenger and one by registered mail, and one list is deposited with the Judge of the nearest United States court. This is to insure absolute safety and accuracy of the record.

The President of the Senate, in the presence of the Senate and the House of Representatives, opens the lists, and the votes are counted. If any candidate has a majority vote, he is declared elected. Usually, one candidate has a majority. If no person has a majority, the House of Representatives elects the President from the two or three highest on the list. When the House of Representatives votes for President the vote is by states, the representation from each state having one vote.

In 1800 no candidate for President had a majority. The House of Representatives had to decide whether John Adams, Thomas Jefferson, or Aaron Burr should be President. Thomas Jefferson was elected. In 1824 the House of Representatives was called upon to decide between John Quincy Adams and Andrew Jackson. Adams was elected. An Electoral Commission appointed by Congress decided the disputed election of 1876, voting in favor of Rutherford B. Hayes. Hayes' opponent was Samuel J. Tilden. The question at issue was that of illegal voting in one of the Southern states.

The President formerly took office on the fourth day of March following his election. The Twentieth Amendment to the Constitution changed the date to January 20.

QUESTIONS AND ANSWERS

1. *Q.* Who is the Chief Executive of the United States?
   A. The President is the Chief Executive. He serves four years.

2. *Q.* What are the qualifications of the President?
    A. He must be a natural-born citizen, at least thirty-five years of age, and a resident of the United States for fourteen years preceding this election.

3. *Q.* What are some of the President's powers and duties?
    A. He signs and vetoes bills; he is Commander-in-Chief of the Army and Navy; he delivers an annual message to Congress; he makes treaties and appoints certain officers with the consent of the Senate.

4. *Q.* How is the President elected?
    A. The President is elected by the people, but not directly. The people elect Presidential electors and the Presidential electors elect the President.

5. *Q.* How many Presidential electors does any state have?
    A. The number of Presidential electors in a state is equal to the number of Representatives from that state plus the number of United States Senators. Members of Congress do not serve as Presidential electors.

6. *Q.* What is the total number of Presidential electors?
    A. As there are 435 Representatives, 100 United States Senators and 3 Electors from the District of Columbia, there are a total of 538 Presidential electors. We usually speak of the entire number of Presidential electors as the electoral college.

7. *Q.* When is the President elected?
    A. The Presidential electors are chosen in November every fourth year. These electors meet at their state capitals in December and elect the President. To elect requires a majority of the 538 Presidential electors.

8. *Q.* Who elects a President if the Presidential electors fail to do so?
    A. In that case the House of Representatives must elect the President. The representation from each state has one vote.

9. *Q.* What Presidents were elected by the House of Representatives?
    A. Thomas Jefferson and John Quincy Adams were elected by the House of Representatives. The disputed election of 1876 was decided by an Electoral Commission, appointed by Congress. Rutherford B. Hayes was declared President.

10. *Q.* How are the candidates for Presidential electors selected?
    A. Political parties, such as Republicans, Democrats, Socialists and Prohibitionists, form state organizations. The leaders of these organizations choose the men and women for whom the voters cast their ballots.

11. *Q.* What is the present order of succession to the Presidency?
    A. President, Vice-President, Speaker of the House of Representatives, President *pro tem* of the United States Senate, Secretary of State, Secretary of the Treasury, other Cabinet officers, if qualified.

LESSON XII

THE PRESIDENT'S CABINET

The Cabinet is a body of official advisors appointed by the President with the consent of the Senate, to assist in the executive work of the United States government. There are 14 departments in the Cabinet, many of them having several divisions called Bureaus. The heads of the departments are the chief advisors to the President. In the following list the Cabinet officers are arranged in the order in which they will succeed to the Presidency, if eligible.

1. Secretary of State—James Baker
2. Secretary of the Treasury—Nicholas Brady
3. Secretary of the Defense—Richard Cheney
4. Attorney General—Richard Thornburgh
5. Secretary of the Interior—Manuel Lujan
6. Secretary of Agriculture—Edward Madigan
7. Secretary of Commerce—Robert Mosbacher
8. Secretary of Labor—Lynn Martin
9. Secretary of Health and Human Services—Louis Sullivan
10. Secretary of Housing and Urban Development—Jack Kemp
11. Secretary of Transportation—Samuel Skinner
12. Secretary of Energy—James Watkins
13. Secretary of Education—Lamar Alexander
14. Secretary of Veterans' Affairs—Edward Derwinski

The duties of the Cabinet officers are as follows:

1. The Secretary of State has charge of our diplomatic relations with foreign countries. The control of passports and the relations with consuls and ambassadors come under his department.

2. The Secretary of the Treasury has charge of the financial affairs of the United States. Included in this department are, also, the Bureau of Engraving and Printing, the control of Mints, the United States Secret Service, and Internal Revenue (including income tax).

3. The Secretary of National Defense is the head of a department which consolidates the affairs of Army, Air Forces, and Navy (including Marines). Three Assistant Secretaries have been appointed to head these divisions. This department is responsible for approximately two and one-half million men.

4. The Attorney General, whose department is often called the Department of Justice, is the United States lawyer. He is the legal adviser of the other Cabinet members. He has charge of United States prisons. The Bureau of Immigration and the Bureau of Naturalization are included in this department.

5. The Secretary of the Interior has charge of many important affairs within the United States. Among the departments are the Bureau of Mines, Office of Indian Affairs, National Park Service, and Fish and Wildlife Service.

6. The Secretary of Agriculture has charge of the improvement of agricultural conditions. The Bureau of Soils, the Bureau of Markets, the Forest Service, the Dairy Industry and Plant Quarantine are among the important divisions of this department.

7. The Secretary of Commerce has charge of our trade relations at home and abroad. Some of the divisions are the Bureau of Foreign and Domestic Commerce, Census Bureau, Patent Office, Bureau of Public Roads and Weather Bureau.

8. The Secretary of Labor has charge of important affairs concerning Labor. Included in this department are the Bureau of Labor Statistics, and Veterans' Reemployment Rights.

9. The Secretary of Health and Human Services is in charge of the Social Security Administration, Public Health Service, Children's Bureau, and Women's Bureau.

10. The Secretary of Housing and Urban Development supervises and coordinates various organizations dealing with housing construction and financing such as the Federal Housing Administration (FHA) and the Federal National Mortgage Association (FNMA).

11. The Secretary of Transportation supervises and coordinates activities of the National Transportation Safety Board, U.S. Coast Guard, Federal Aviation Administration, Federal Highway Administration, Federal Railroad Administration and the St. Lawrence Seaway Development Corporation.

12.   The Secretary of Energy supervises and coordinates the following agencies: the Federal Energy Board, the Energy Research and Development Administration, the Federal Power Commission, as well as portions of other departments and agencies formerly included in other departments.

13.   The Secretary of Education supervises all the committees concerned with education.

QUESTIONS

1.   Q.   What is the Cabinet?
      A.   The Cabinet is a body of persons who assist the President in his executive duties.
2.   Q.   How do Cabinet officers get their positions?
      A.   They are appointed by the President with the consent of the Senate.
3.   Q.   Who is the head of the Cabinet?
      A.   The Secretary of State is head of the Cabinet.
4.   Q.   Which Cabinet officer has charge of naturalization?
      A.   The Department of Justice, under the Attorney General, now has charge of the Bureau of Naturalization and Immigration.
5.   Q.   Is it necessary that a Cabinet officer be a native-born citizen of the United States?
      A.   It is not necessary. A naturalized citizen may hold a Cabinet office. He cannot, however, succeed to the Presidency.

LESSON XIII

THE JUDICIAL BRANCH OF THE NATIONAL GOVERNMENT

Judicial means law-interpreting or law-explaining. The judicial branch of the United States government includes all United States courts. United States courts are usually called Federal Courts.

The Constitution established the United States Supreme Court and gave Congress power to establish any other courts that might be found necessary.

The Supreme Court is the highest Federal Court. It consists of nine judges. The head judge is called the Chief Justice and the others are Associate Justices. The judges are appointed by the President, with the consent of the Senate. They serve for life, or during good behavior.

The Supreme Court meets in the Supreme Court Building at Washington, D.C. It tries only the most important cases. Any case involving the United States Constitution is tried in this court. For example, if there is a question as to whether some law agrees with the principles of the Constitution, the Supreme Court will decide the matter. Cases are often appealed from the Appellate Courts.

Congress has established eleven Circuit Courts of Appeal. Included in the Ninth Circuit are Montana, California, Arizona, Nevada, Oregon, Washington, Idaho, Alaska, Hawaii, and Guam.

Congress has established ninety-one District Courts. The number increases with the growth of population. The District Courts try such cases as post office or postal offenses, "bootlegging," when it involves United States laws, and cases involving United States soldiers and sailors. If the cases are not settled in the District Courts they may go to the Circuit Court of Appeals.

There are in addition special courts; for example: The U.S. Court of Claims, the U.S. Court of Customs and Patent Appeals, and Territorial Courts.

QUESTIONS

1. *Q.* What is the Judicial branch of the United States government?
   A. The Judicial branch of the United States government includes all the United States courts. They are called Federal courts.
2. *Q.* What is the highest Federal Court?
   A. The Supreme Court is the highest Federal court.

3. *Q.* How is the Supreme Court composed?
   A. The Supreme Court consists of nine members: one Chief Justice and eight Associate Justices. They are appointed by the President, with the consent of the Senate. They serve for life, or during good behavior, so that they may be independent in making their decisions.
4. *Q.* Who is the head of the Supreme Court?
   A. Judge William Rehnquist is now Chief Justice.
5. *Q.* What other Federal Courts are there?
   A. There are 11 Circuit Courts of Appeal and 91 District Courts. Four of the District Courts are in California.
6. *Q.* Where would a post office case be tried?
   A. It would be tried in the nearest United States District Court.
7. *Q.* What special United States courts are there?
   A. The U.S. Court of Claims, U.S. Court of Customs and Patent Appeals, Territorial Courts and others.
8. *Q.* Who are the Associate Justices of the United States Supreme Court?
   A. The Associate Judges are: Judges Stevens, White, Marshall, Blackmun, O'Conner, Scalia, Kennedy, and Souter.
9. *Q.* What does the word Federal mean?
   A. Federal means national. A Federal officer is a United States officer; a Federal building is a United States building; a Federal law is a United States law, the Federal government is the United States government.
10. *Q.* If Congress passes a law which does not agree with some principle of the constitution, must such a law go into effect?
    A. Yes. If there is a question in regard to the constitutionality of a law, it may be appealed to the United States Supreme Court for decision. Some years ago there was strong opposition to the NRA ("Blue Eagle") law. An appeal was made to the Supreme Court, which decided the law was unconstitutional.
11. *Q.* Why does the United States have three branches of government instead of giving all the responsibility to one branch?
    A. One branch with full power would have too much authority and responsibility. Three branches are more democratic. When there are three branches each acts as a check and balance for the others. For example, when the President vetoes a bill it must be carefully reconsidered by Congress in the light of his objections, and a two-thirds majority vote is required for its passage. Thus, the executive branch acts as a check upon the legislative branch. The Supreme Court checks both legislative and executive branches.

LESSON XIV

AMENDMENTS

The Constitution of the United States is the supreme law of the nation. It was so well planned in the beginning that comparatively few changes have been found necessary. Changes in the Constitution are called amendments. Amendments are made in somewhat the same way as laws, but they do not go to the President to be signed. They are voted upon by the legislatures of the states, instead.

The usual way of making an amendment is as follows:

An amendment must pass both houses of Congress by a two-thirds majority vote. It must then be ratified by the legislatures of three-fourths of the states.

Amendments may be proposed by a convention called by Congress at the request of the states. This method has never been used.

Twenty-six amendments have been passed by Congress and ratified by the states. The first ten amendments were passed in 1791. These ten amendments are called the "Bill of Rights."

The substance of the amendments to the Constitution is as follows:

Amendment I guarantees freedom of speech, freedom of religion, freedom of the press, and the right of peaceable assembly and petition. Amendments II to X guarantee other rights: the right to a fair and speedy trial; the right of trial by jury; the right to have bail; the right to security in the home.

Amendment XI defines the authority of the United States judicial department in connection with suits against a state. Amendment XII tells how the President is elected. Amendments XIII, XIV, and XV came as a result of the Civil War. Amendment XIII forbids slavery. Amendment XIV makes the former slaves citizens, defines citizenship, and fixes the penalty for depriving citizens of their citizenship rights. Amendment XV gives former slaves and their descendants the right to vote. Amendment XVI gives Congress power to lay income taxes. Amendment XVII gives the people the right to elect United States Senators. Formerly the Senators were elected by the state legislatures. Amendment XVIII established National Prohibition. Amendment XIX grants National Woman Suffrage.

Amendment XX provides that the President will be inaugurated on January 20, instead of March 4; that Congress shall meet on January 3, instead of the first Monday in December; that the terms of members of Congress shall begin on January 3; that if the President-elect dies before inauguration, the Vice-President-elect shall become President.

Amendment XXI repeals National Prohibition.

Amendment XXII provides that no President shall be elected for more than two terms.

Amendment XXIII, ratified in March, 1961, permits citizens of the District of Columbia, for the first time, to vote for President and Vice-President in National Elections. The District was given three votes in the Electoral College but continues to be without representation in Congress.

Amendment XXIV was ratified by three-fourths of the States on January 23, 1964. It abolished poll taxes or other voting taxes in elections for President, Vice-President, Senators or Representatives in Congress.

Amendment XXV, ratified February 10, 1967, covers the problems of Succession to the Presidency and Vice Presidency and disability of the President.

Amendment XXVI, ratified June 30, 1971, changes the voting age from twenty-one to eighteen years.

QUESTIONS

1. Q. What is an amendment?
   A. An amendment is a change in the Constitution, or an addition to the Constitution.
2. Q. How is an amendment usually made?
   A. An amendment must pass both houses of Congress by a two-thirds majority vote, and must then be ratified by the legislatures of three-fourths of the states.
3. Q. Does the President sign amendments?
   A. The President neither signs nor vetoes amendments. They are not submitted to him.
4. Q. How many amendments have been made to the constitution?
   A. Twenty-six amendments have been made.
5. Q. What are the first ten amendments called?
   A. The first ten amendments are called the "Bill of Rights." They safeguard our inherent rights by prohibiting Congress from ever passing laws to take away or abridge these rights. They guarantee us the right to freedom of speech, freedom of religion, freedom of the press, the right of peaceable assembly and petition, the right to security in the home, the right to a jury trial, and other essential rights.

LESSON XV

LEGISLATIVE BRANCH OF THE STATE

Just as the United States Constitution is the "supreme law of the United States," so too each of the fifty states has a constitution of its own which is the supreme law of that particular state. The only restriction on the state constitutions is that they must not conflict with the United States Constitution. State governments are similar to national government in that there are three general branches of government. These are the legislative branch (to make laws), the executive branch (to enforce the laws) and the judicial branch (to explain and apply the laws).

The law-making or legislative branch of the state government is usually called a state legislature or state assembly. In every state except Nebraska, it is divided into two groups or "houses." The upper house is usually called the Senate and the members of that house, called state senators, are usually elected for a four-year term. The members of the lower house, which may be known as the State House of Representatives, or State Assembly, usually serve for two-year terms.

Since 1934, the Nebraska legislature has had only one house composed of forty-three members called "legislators." This is known as a *unicameral* legislature which means that it is made up of "one chamber."

Any legislator who desires to make a new law presents a document to the particular house to which he belongs. This document is known as a "bill." If the bill is passed by the house in which it is introduced, it goes to the other house for approval. After it passes both houses, it goes to the governor of the state for his signature. In every state, except North Carolina, the governor may veto the bill (which means that he disapproves it). If he vetoes it or refuses to sign it, the bill will not become a state law unless the legislators vote on the bill again and decide to pass it without the governor's approval. Most state laws require a two-thirds vote of the members of each house of the legislature in order to pass a law after the governor has vetoed the bill.

QUESTIONS

1. *Q.* What is the legislative branch of the state?
    A. The legislative branch of the state is the State Legislature or State Assembly.

2. Q. What are the divisions of the State Legislatures?
    A. Most State Legislatures are divided into two houses: the State Senate and the Assembly or State House of Representatives.
3. Q. How does the State Legislature make laws?
    A. State laws are made by the Legislature in the same way that national laws are made by Congress. In the state the Governor acts instead of the President.

LESSON XVI

EXECUTIVE BRANCH OF THE STATE

The Chief Executive of the state is the Governor. He is elected by the voters. His powers and duties correspond to those of the President of the United States. The Governor sees that laws are enforced, signs or vetoes bills, appoints certain officers and boards, grants pardons, reprieves and commutations, may call special sessions of the legislature, and is Commander-in-Chief of the state militia.

A Lieutenant Governor, corresponding to the Vice-President of the United States, is also elected by the voters. He presides over the State Senate, and takes the place of the Governor whenever necessary.

Other state officers who are usually elected by the people include: Secretary of State, State Treasurer, Attorney General, State Controller or Auditor and State Superintendent of Schools.

In many of the states, including California, state officers are elected for four-year terms. Some states, however, hold elections for these positions every two years.

In most states there is a group corresponding to the President's Cabinet which assists the Governor in making decisions of importance to the people of the state. This group is made up of the heads of important state departments. The members of this group are usually appointed by the Governor and changes are more frequent than in the President's Cabinet. In California this group is known as the Governor's Cabinet.

The Executive Branch of State Government also includes various boards, commissions or departments with specialized powers and functions. Usually the members of these groups are appointed by the Governor but in some cases they are elected by the voters.

Typical State Boards or Commissions are: Board of Health, Board of Education, Board of Prison Directors, State Tax Commission, Department of Social Welfare, Department of Finance, State Aeronautics Commission, and Personnel Board.

In California the State Board of Equalization, which is composed of four members, is elected by the voters every four years. One man is selected from each of four districts within the state, by the voters who reside within that district.

1. *Q.* Who is the Chief Executive of the State?
   A. The Governor is the Chief Executive. His powers and duties correspond to those of the President of the United States. In California his term of office is four years. George Deukmejian was elected governor in November, 1982 and again in November, 1986 to serve another four-year term.
2. *Q.* What officer corresponds to the Vice-President?
   A. The Lieutenant Governor. He is the presiding officer of the State Senate.
3. *Q.* What is the Governor's Cabinet?
   A. The Governor's Cabinet consists of heads of important state departments, most of whom are appointed by the Governor. The Cabinet corresponds to the Cabinet of the President of the United States.
4. *Q.* Name some other State Officers who are usually elected.
   A. The Secretary of State, State Treasurer, Attorney General, State Controller or Auditor and State Superintendent of Schools.
5. *Q.* What are some of the typical Boards, Commissions or Departments which are found in the Executive Department of State Government?
   A. Board of Health, Board of Education, Board of Prison Directors, State Tax Commission, Department of Social Welfare, Department of Finance, State Aeronautics Commission, and State Personnel Board.

LESSON XVII

JUDICIAL BRANCH OF THE STATE

The Judicial branch of California includes state courts, county courts, city, village and township courts.

The highest court is the State Supreme Court, which consists of seven judges: a Chief Justice and six Associate Justices. These judges are elected by the people and hold office twelve years. They try the most important cases in the state, including all which have to do with the state constitution. The Supreme Court also tries certain cases which have been appealed from the lower courts.

Below the Supreme Court are the Courts of Appeal which are divided amoung six Appellate districts: 1. San Francisco; 2. Los Angeles; 3. Sacramento; 4. San Diego; 5. Fresno; 6. San Jose. These courts are principally concerned with appeals from the Superior Courts.

Each county in the state has a Superior Court. The Superior Court is the county court. The populous counties usually have several departments in the Superior Court. The judges in the Superior Courts are elected by the people and serve six years. Most of the common cases are tried in the Superior Court, except such small cases as may be settled in the lower courts.

Among the cases frequently tried in the Superior Court are: divorces, cases involving land, money, or other property; burglary, embezzlement, murder, serious assault, and many others.

A local court reorganization went into effect on January 1, 1952. Large cities, or combinations of larger communities, have Municipal Courts. Smaller communities, or combinations, have Justice Courts. In these courts minor cases, such as disorderly conduct, drunkenness, vagrancy, automobile speeding, breaking of local ordinances, and small property cases, are usually tried and settled.

Preliminary trials for more serious offenses, such as murder or burglary, are also held in the local courts. If the evidence warrants, the accused person is then "bound over" for trial in the Superior Court, and is either released on bail or imprisoned in the county jail until his trial takes place.

Every part of the United States, even the most remote spot in the mountains or wilderness, is within the jurisdiction of some court. The Judicial department of our government extends its protection to all.

QUESTIONS

1. **Q.** What is the Judicial branch of the state?
   A. The Judicial branch includes all state courts.
2. **Q.** What is the highest court in the State of California?
   A. The highest court is the State Supreme Court, which consists of a Chief Justice and six Associate Justices, elected by the people for terms of twelve years.
3. **Q.** What are the county courts?
   A. Each county in the state has a Superior Court.
4. **Q.** What local courts has California?
   A. Cities, or combinations of cities, have Municipal Courts. Smaller communities have Justice's Courts. A new organization of these courts went into effect on January 1, 1952.
5. **Q.** Has California any state courts in addition to the State Supreme Court?
   A. Yes, California has District Courts of Appeal divided among six Appelate districts.
6. **Q.** How do the judges of the Courts of Appeal secure their positions?
   A. The judges of the Courts of Appeal are elected by the voters of the districts in which they hold court. The term of office is twelve years.

At the conclusion of a term a judge may be a candidate for the office again if he wishes, and if he takes the proper nomination procedures. Voters will vote "YES" or "NO" on his candidacy.

If a judge decides to be a candidate to succeed himself, no candidate may run against him. Should he be rejected by the voters (a majority of "NO" votes), the Governor appoints a judge to fill the vacancy until the next regular election. The judge who failed of election cannot be a candidate at the next election.

LESSON XVIII

COUNTY GOVERNMENT

Each of the states of the United States is divided into smaller districts called "counties" with the exception of Louisiana, where they are called "parishes." In each county there is one town or city which is the headquarters of the county government and is known as the "County Seat."

County governments are usually run by a Board of Supervisors or a Board of County Commissioners. The members of the Board are elected by the voters of the county usually for four-year terms. The number of members on most county boards is an odd number, varying from five to eleven people.

County governments usually get their power and authority from the state constitution, and they carry out state laws within the district under their control. They deal with such matters as schools, hospital and welfare services, highway construction and maintenance, assessment and collection of taxes, law enforcement and many other functions. Counties differ from cities in that cities are more concerned with providing special services, such as police, fire and health protection to the people who live in the cities.

In recent years, some of the larger counties have adopted the plan of employing a county manager or county administrator, whose duties are similar to those of the manager of a business. This man is usually appointed and paid by the county board and performs his work under the authority and control of the board. He attends to the routine duties and problems which arise from day to day in connection with the county government, and which are necessary to keep the government running. His duties, for example, might include the right to hire and fire county workers, to supervise county purchases, to arrange for space for additional county offices and any number of similar jobs.

Every county has a court of law which is usually known as the County Court or Superior Court and is located at the court house in the County Seat. Additional courts called Municipal Courts, Justice Courts, Police Courts or City Courts are maintained to try less important cases and are usually located in the outlying areas of the county.

In addition to the county board, there are certain other county officers who help do the work of the county government. Some of these people are elected by the voters; others are appointed either by the county board, the governor of the state or the state legislature. They normally perform the following duties:

1. The County Clerk. He issues marriage licenses and naturalization papers. He has charge of election returns.

2. The County Treasurer. He receives and pays out the county money.

3. The County Tax Collector. He collects the county taxes.

4. The County Assessor. He assesses property for county taxation purposes.

5. The County Recorder. He keeps a record of deeds, mortgages, and transfers of property.

6. The County Auditor. He audits the accounts of the other county officers. He issues warrants for county money.

7. The County Superintendent of Schools. He has general charge of all schools in the county except those in established cities.

8. The County Surveyor. He surveys county lines and boundaries.

9. The County Coroner. He investigates accidental and suspicious deaths.

10. The Public Administrator. He probates estates when there is no executor or qualified relative.

11. The District Attorney. He represents the county in the prosecution of cases. He is the county lawyer.

In many of the smaller counties one person may hold several county offices and perform all of the duties connected with each office.

SPECIAL DISTRICTS

Many times people who reside in one part of the county decide that they need or would like to have some services which are not being furnished by the county government. Most states have laws which make it possible for these people to organize special districts to provide, for example, fire protection, sewage disposal, establish hospitals or set up new schools. Under these laws the residents in the district can petition the county board to establish the district, and the county board will then allow the voters in the district to vote upon the proposal at the next election. If the plan passes then, the residents within the district have to pay additional taxes to pay for the cost of setting up and operating the district for their benefit.

Some districts are operated directly under the county board. In others, however, a separate district board is selected from residents of the district by the voters in the district.

QUESTIONS

1. Q. What is the Legislative branch of the county government?
   A. The legislative branch of the county government is the County Board of Supervisors.
2. Q. How many members are there in the County Board of Supervisors?
   A. There are five members usually. San Francisco County has eleven.

3. *Q.* What is the Executive branch of county government?
   A. The County Board of Supervisors and the Sheriff have executive authority.
4. *Q.* What is the Judicial branch of the county government?
   A. The Superior Court is the Judicial branch of the county government.
5. *Q.* What are the other county officers?
   A. They are the County Clerk, County Treasurer, County Auditor, County Tax Collector, County Surveyor, County Coroner, County Sheriff, County Superintendent of Schools, County Board of Supervisors, District Attorney, Public Administrator, and Superior Judge. In small counties one person frequently holds two or more offices. There are also certain appointive county officials, such as the County Librarian, the County Health Officer, and others.

LESSON XIX

A TYPICAL COUNTY

Alameda County, which is located on the east shore of San Francisco Bay, has a population in excess of 1,000,000 people and is one of the largest of the 58 counties in California. Historically it was divided into seven townships: Alameda, Brooklyn, Eden, Murray, Oakland, Pleasanton and Washington.

In recent years the cities of Berkeley, Albany, Emeryville and Piedmont were combined into an eighth township — Peralta. Other cities in the county include Oakland (the County Seat), Alameda, San Leandro, Hayward, Fremont, Newark, Union City, Pleasanton and Livermore.

Alameda County includes all of two State Senate districts (8 and 9) and a portion of a third (11). There are five assembly districts in the county which are numbered 12 to 15 inclusive and 25.

For purposes of government, the county is divided into five supervisorial districts. Voters within each of those districts elect a person who must be a resident of the district to be their supervisor for a four-year term

Other elective county officers are the following: Assessor, Auditor, Clerk and Recorder, District Attorney, Superintendent of Schools, Sheriff, Tax Collector and Treasurer, and Administrator.

Additional county officers who are appointed by the Board of Supervisors include the following:

Purchasing Agent, Farm Advisor, Adult Probation Officer, County Librarian, Superintendent of County Hospital, Coroner, and Surveyor.

There are many special districts in Alameda County. These include elementary school districts, fire protection districts, sanitary districts, park, recreation and parkway districts, and many other types.

The Judicial branch of the county consists of the Superior Court, Municipal Courts and Justice Courts. The Superior Court has 37 departments.

A statewide court reorganization law which went into effect in 1952 established Municipal Courts. There are five Municipal Court Judicial Districts in Alameda County—Alameda, Berkeley-Albany, Oakland-Piedmont, Hayward, Fremont-Newark-Union City, and Livermore-Pleasanton. In addition there are two Justice Court Districts which are located at Livermore and Pleasanton.

QUESTIONS

1. What is the name of the governing board of your county?
2. How many members are on the board?
3. What are the names of the members?
4. What is the county seat in your county?
5. What other officials in your county are elected by the voters?
6. What are your county courts?
7. Are there any "special districts" which operate within your county? If so, name three of them.
8. Who are your State Senators? Your State Assemblyman or Representative? Your Congressman?

LESSON XX

CITY ORGANIZATION AND GOVERNMENT

Cities in California are grouped according to their population into six classes. Cities of the first class include those having above 500,000 inhabitants. Cities of the sixth class include all those whose population is below 6,000. Cities of the second, third, fourth, and fifth classes, with subdivisions, lie between these two units.

The organization of a city government permits of greater variety than does that of a county. Cities may choose from several different forms of government.

California cities have as their governing boards Commissioners or Councilmen (sometimes called Trustees). San Francisco, city and county united, has a Board of Supervisors.

Cities which have the City Manager plan include Avalon, Alameda, Bakersfield, Berkeley, Burbank, Chico, Claremont, Compton, Coronado, El Cerrito, Fillmore, Glendale, Hanford, Hawthorne, Hayward, Hemet, Hillsborough, Lodi, Long Beach, Manhattan Beach, Merced, Monterey, Monterey Park, Modesto, Napa, National City, Oakland, Pacific Grove, Palm Springs, Palo Alto, Pasadena, Petaluma, Porterville, Redding, Redlands, Redondo Beach, Redwood City, Richmond, Sacramento, Salinas, San Carlos, San Diego, San Jose, San Leandro, San Mateo, San Rafael, Santa Cruz, Santa Monica, Santa Rosa, South Pasadena, South San Francisco, Stockton, Tulare, Upland, Vallejo, Visalia, Whittier, Woodland.

A number of cities have City Administrators, whose duties correspond to those of the City Managers.

The constitution of a city is called a charter. The city, like the nation, the state, and the county, has three departments of government.

The Chief Executive of a city is called the Mayor. The legislative branch of a city is usually the City Council or the Board of Supervisors. The judicial branch of a city consists of the Police Courts and Justice Courts.

Among the usual city officers are the Treasurer, Tax Collector, Assessor, Auditor, Health Officer, Clerk, Engineer, Police Chief, Fire Chief, and several minor officers. Some of these officers are elected by the voters and others are appointed by the Mayor.

City laws are called ordinances. Among the well-known ordinances in cities are the automobile regulation ordinances, bicycle-riding ordinances, milk-delivery ordinances, ordinances regulating the disposal of domestic animals, building ordinances, and health ordinances. These ordinances differ in various communities, in accordance with the wishes of the citizens.

QUESTIONS

1. Q. What is the constitution of a city called?
    A. The constitution of a city is called a charter.
2. Q. Who is the Chief Executive of a city?
    A. The Chief Executive of a city is the Mayor.
3. Q. What is the legislative branch of a city?
    A. The legislative branch of a city is usually the City Council. In San Francisco city and county it is the Board of Supervisors.
4. Q. What is the judicial branch of a city?
    A. The judicial branch of a city is the Police Court or Justice Court, or both. City Courts are usually called Municipal Courts.
5. Q. What are city laws called?
    A. City laws are called ordinances.
6. Q. What are some common ordinances?
    A. Most communities have ordinances regulating the speed of automobiles, the riding of bicycles on sidewalks, the disposal of garbage, the construction of buildings, and the issuing of licenses.

LESSON XXI

SUFFRAGE

Suffrage means the right to vote. The privilege of suffrage is one of the greatest blessings of a democracy. Every citizen should consider it his duty to vote for the officers and measures that he thinks best for the country. It is greatly to be regretted that many people neglect this important duty.

The United States Constitution does not specify any uniform voting age. Until recently, all states had established twenty-one years as the age to be attained before voting. In 1970 Congress passed a law establishing 18 years as the legal voting age.

A voter in California must have four qualifications: he must be a citizen of the United States; he must be at least eighteen years old; he must have lived in the county at least ninety days; he must have lived in his precinct at least fifty-four days.

By State laws voting rights may be denied to certain classes of citizens. In California these include mental imcompetents, persons convicted of major crimes (felonies), and persons who bet on elections. (The law against betting on elections is rarely enforced.)

When a person wishes to become a candidate for public office in this state a "Declaration of Candidacy" must be filed with the County Clerk or Registrar of Voters. The candidate may file this in person, or it may be filed by five electors of any political party, followed by the acceptance of the candidate. Following the declaration of candidacy, the candidate has verification deputies appointed to secure signatures of sponsors for his nomination. The number of sponsors required depends upon the nature of the office.

All declarations of candidacy and sponsors' certificates must be filed with the Secretary of State not more than 90 days nor less than 60 days before the June primary election. When this procedure is completed, the name of the candidate is printed upon the primary ballot. At the primary election the candidate of each political party receiving the highest vote for each office becomes the political party's candidate at the general election. For non-partisan offices the two candidates who receive the highest votes at the primary election become candidates for each such office at the general election. This method is for state offices. Different systems may be used in some cities of the state, as may be provided for in such city charters.

In California people must register before they may vote. In order to vote at a primary election, the person who registers must tell to what political party he belongs, if any. He may register as Non-Partisan.

The chief political parties in the United States are the Republicans and Democrats.

These parties have many points in common. They all believe in a government "of the people, by the people, and for the people." They differ in some important respects.

In general, the Democrats are thought to be liberal and the Republicans conservative.

When a person applies for citizenship in this country he must swear that he does not believe in polygamy or anarchy.

Polygamy is the practice of having more than one wife or husband at the same time. This is not legal in the United States.

An anarchist is a person who does not believe in organized government. Anarchists, Communists, and other radicals have sometimes made a great deal of disturbance in the United States by urging resistance to laws, destroying of property, and the overthrow of government.

There are undoubtedly some features of our government that may be improved. It is important that every qualified resident of this country be an intelligent, thoughtful citizen, who will vote for the right officers and laws to correct evils that may exist.

The Eighteenth Amendment to the United States Constitution established national prohibition. The amendment was violated in many parts of the country by people who argued that, because they did not believe in prohibition, they need not keep the prohibition law. The good citizen obeys the law, while it is a law, whether he approves of it or not. And if he feels it is a poor law, he works through legal channels to have it changed.

DEMOCRACY

Democracy is any form of government by the people. There are "pure democracies" and "representative democracies." In the early days of New England all the voters of a township met, and enacted legislation for the township. This was *pure* democracy, all voters taking part.

Most democracies are representative democracies. A democracy in which the people elect representatives to serve for them, and elect a President as Chief Executive is called a republic. The United States, Mexico, Switzerland, and some of the nations of South America and Central America are republics.

Iceland became a republic in 1944. The Republic of the Philippines was formally established on July 4, 1946.

In a "monarchistic democracy" the people elect representatives to make laws, but the executive officer, a king or queen, inherits the position of ruler. Great Britain, Sweden, Denmark, Holland, and Belgium are democracies of this type. In these nations representatives elected by the voters have legislative powers, but they do not elect their ruler.

COMMUNISM

Communism differs from democracy in several ways. There is only one political party and all the people must belong to it. Citizens are not allowed to criticize the government publicly. Freedom of speech and press do not exist and religion is minimized. Individual enterprise is not encouraged, and major industries are run by the government. After World War II there was poor communication between the U.S. and the major Communist countries, Russia and the People's Republic of China. In his first term President Nixon traveled to both these countries and attempted to improve our relations with them. At the present time our relations with them are vastly improved. All seem dedicated to the prevention of World War. In 1978 the United States recognized the People's Republic of China as the true Chinese government.

FASCISM

Fascism is a form of government in which all power is held by a small ruling group headed by one person who is called a dictator. The term "Fascism" was first used by Mussolini at the time he became dictator of Italy in 1922. Germany, under Hitler, was also a Fascist Government.

Under Fascism the dictator controls education, the press and radio, religion, art, and the entire economic and political life of the country. There is no freedom of speech or press and individual rights are abolished.

During the periods of Fascist control, Italy and Germany were "Police States."

QUESTIONS

1. *Q.* What are the necessary qualifications for a voter in California?
   A. A voter must be a citizen, at least eighteen years of age, at least ninety days a resident of the county, and fifty-four days a resident of the precinct.

2. *Q.* What is a primary election?
   A. A primary election is an election held for the purpose of nominating condidates for office. Primary elections in California were held in June 1988. At these elections political parties nominated their candidates to contest in the final election held in November 1988.

3. *Q.* What are the chief political parties in the United States?
   A. Republican and Democrat.
4. *Q.* What is polygamy?
   A. Polygamy is the practice of plural marriage.
5. *Q.* What is an anarchist?
   A. An anarchist is a person who believes in the overthrow of organized government.
6. *Q.* When a candidate for citizenship takes his naturalization examination, he is asked these questions, "Are you a Communist? Have you been a Communist or a member of any other subversive organization within the past ten years?" Why are these questions asked?
   A. An alien, in becoming a citizen, must swear that he believes in our government as established by the Constitution of the United States, and that he will be loyal to that government and obey its laws.

   A Communist does not believe in the present government of the United States, and, therefore, cannot truthfully take the oath of allegiance. If a candidate is a Communist and denies the fact in becoming a citizen, he commits perjury.
7. *Q.* Does the Declaration of Independence say anything against dictators?
   A. The Declaration of Independence says, "All men are created equal . . . with certain inalienable rights. To secure these rights governments are instituted among men, deriving their just powers from the consent of the governed." A dictator does not derive his powers from the consent of the governed.

LESSON XXII

OUR COUNTRY'S WARS

Americans are justly proud of the fact that the declared wars in which our country has been engaged have been wars waged in behalf of freedom and right. The thousands of American soldiers who have given their lives in these battles have not died in vain. Every declared conflict has resulted in a victory for the cause which our country championed. Not only have our own people secured and maintained their independence, but the people of many other countries have gained freedom through the help that the United States has given.

The United States has been engaged in the following wars:

1. *The Revolutionary War,* 1775-1783.

Countries engaged: Thirteen Colonies (afterward known as United States) against Great Britain. The colonies were assisted by France.

Cause: "Taxation without representation."

Result: The United States secured its independence.

Leaders — American: George Washington, Patrick Henry, Nathaniel Greene, Thomas Jefferson, Benjamin Franklin, Marquis de Lafayette.

2. *The War of 1812,* 1812-1814.

Countries engaged: United States and Great Britain.

Cause: Trouble in regard to "the freedom of the seas."

Result: United States won commercial independence.

Leaders — American: Commodore Perry, General Andrew Jackson.

3. *The Mexican War,* 1846-1848.

Countries engaged: United States and Mexico

Cause: Dispute over the boundary line between the two countries.

Result: Settlement of boundary line. Addition of New Mexico and California to United States territory.

Leaders — American: General Zachary Taylor, John C. Fremont, General Kearney, General Winfield Scott.

4. *The Civil War,* 1861-1865.

Country engaged: The Northern states of United States and the Southern states.

Cause: The slavery question and the doctrine of "States' rights."

Results: The abolition of slavery. The preservation of the Union.

Leaders — Federal: Abraham Lincoln (President), General Grant, General Sherman, General Sheridan, General McClellan, General Mead.

Confederate — Jefferson Davis (President), General Robert E. Lee, "Stonewall" Jackson, General Joseph E. Johnston.

5. *The Spanish-American War,* 1898.

Countries engaged: United States and Spain.

Cause: Spanish tyranny in Cuba. The blowing up of the United States battleship *Maine.*

Results: Puerto Rico, Guam, and the Philippines were ceded to United States by Spain. Cuba became independent.

Leaders — American: William McKinley (President), Admiral Dewey, Colonel Theodore Roosevelt, Admiral Sampson, Commodore Schley, General Wood, General Miles.

6. *World War I,* 1917-1918.

Countries engaged: Great Britain, France, and their Allies against Germany and her Allies.

Cause: Germany's ambition for power and expansion of territory.

Result: The curbing of Germany's ambition. The overthrow of the German government. The liberation of several small nations.

Leaders — Allies: Woodrow Wilson (President), General Pershing, Marshal Foch, Marshal Haig.

German-Austrian: Kaiser Wilhelm, Emperor Charles, General von Ludendorff, Marshal von Hindenburg.

7. *World War II,* 1941-1945.

On the morning of December 7, 1941, the Japanese armed forces made an attack upon United States forces at Pearl Harbor, Hawaii. In the afternoon of the same day the Japanese government declared war upon the United States. The following day, December 8, 1941, the United States government declared war upon Japan.

Although Germany had already forcibly occupied several European countries against the protest of the democratic governments, the Second World War really commenced in September, 1939, when Germany attacked Poland. England and France immediately declared war upon Germany. By late 1941, Germany, with the assistance of Italy, had control of practically the entire continent of Europe, and was actively at war with Russia. Japan signed a "non-aggression" pact with Germany and Italy in 1940, and began an insistent demand for a "New Order in East Asia."

In November, 1941, diplomatic representatives of the Japanese government arrived in Washington, D.C., for a conference, ostensibly to maintain peace in the Pacific. While this conference was in progress, the Japanese attack upon Pearl Harbor was made.

On December 11, 1941, Germany and Italy declared war upon the United States. On the same date the United States declared war upon Germany and Italy. The combination of Germany, Italy and Japan was called the "Axis."

The United States government had openly opposed the dictatorship governments of Germany and Italy, and had given aid to the countries seeking to maintain the democratic form of government.

On January 2, 1942, twenty-six nations signed an agreement pledging a fight to the finish against the Axis, and banning any separate peace. The nations made their declaration "convinced that complete victory over their enemies is essential to defend life, liberty, independence, and religious freedom, and to preserve human rights and justice in their own lands as well as in other lands."

Announcement of the pact was made from Washington, D.C., after a conference between President Franklin D. Roosevelt and Prime Minister Winston Churchill of Great Britain.

The nations entering into the cooperative agreement were: The United States, Great Britain, Soviet Russia, China, Australia, Belgium, Canada, Costa Rica, Cuba, Czechoslovakia, the Dominican Republic, Salvador, Greece, Guatemala, Haiti, Honduras, India, Luxemburg, The Netherlands, New Zealand, Nicaragua, Norway, Panama, Poland, South Africa and Yugoslavia.

For nearly four years the Allied Nations and the Axis powers waged a bitter, relentless war on sea and land, involving the whole world, with losses of millions of men and untold millions of dollars in property. The unconditional surrender of Germany on May 7, 1945, and of Japan on September 2, 1945, brought a complete victory to the forces of democracy.

IMPORTANT OFFICIALS IN WORLD WAR II

Commander-in-Chief of Army and Navy — Franklin D. Roosevelt. Succeeded by Harry S. Truman.

Chief of Staff of Armed Forces — General George C. Marshall.

Commander of the entire Fleet — Admiral Ernest H. King.

Commander of Pacific Fleet — Admiral Chester W. Nimitz.

Commander of the Atlantic Fleet — Admiral Royal E. Ingersoll.

Commander of Allied Forces in South Pacific — General Douglas MacArthur.

Supreme Commander of Anglo-American Forces in Europe — General Dwight Eisenhower.

Others — American: Admiral Halsey, Gen. Stilwell, Gen. Patton, Gen. Mark W. Clark, Gen. Chennault, Gen. Lear.

British: Winston Churchill, Gen. Sir Bernard L. Montgomery, Lord Mountbatten, Anthony Eden.

French: Gen. De Gaulle. Russian: Joseph Stalin.

THE UNITED NATIONS

Representatives of fifty Allied Nations met in San Francisco, California, April 15, 1945, as planned by President Roosevelt, to confer on matters of world-wide importance. After more than two months of strenuous work by committees of the delegates, a charter, designed as a basis for securing international peace and cooperation, was presented, discussed, and unanimously adopted. The conference adjourned on June 26, 1945.

Nicaragua was the first nation to report ratification of the Charter. The United States announced its ratification on July 28, 1945. Many other nations followed suit, and the Charter was formally adopted. The organization is now known as the United Nations. One hundred forty nine nations are members. Others are added when qualified.

The United States has been prominent in UN conferences. Loans, equipment, supplies and moral support have been provided for less fortunate nations. Western Europe has been aided by military assistance in Germany and by the Marshall Plan. At the time the United Nations was founded, Nationalist China was one of its members. In 1971 a majority of the delegates to the United Nations voted to include the People's Republic of China and to expel Nationalist China.

NORTH ATLANTIC TREATY ORGANIZATION (NATO)

During the summer of 1949, the United States, Canada and the democracies of Western Europe, twelve nations in all, signed The Atlantic Pact, an agreement guaranteeing mutual cooperation and protection.

UNDECLARED WARS

THE KOREAN CONFLICT

The invasion of Southern Korea by the Communists of Northern Korea in the summer of 1950 was considered by the majority of the United Nations as "an act of aggression," a violation of the charter and the purpose of the United Nations. A determined effort to resist this aggression was made by UN forces, led by the United States, with Gen. MacArthur as Commander of Pacific Forces. The organized resistance was at first successful. The North Korean Communists had been practically defeated when Chinese Communists in overwhelming numbers joined the North Korean forces and drove the UN armies back.

After many months of negotiation, during which the principal point of discussion was the method for handling prisoners of war, an armistice was signed at Panmunjom, Korea, on July 27, 1953. A neutral nations supervisory commission was established.

THE VIETNAM CONFLICT

U.S. participation and action in South Vietnam began with American technical and economic assistance following the Geneva accords that ended the Indo-Chinese War. It escalated into a major effort in 1964 when President Johnson ordered a retaliatory air raid against Communist North Vietnamese P-T boat attacks in the Gulf of Tonkin. Under President Nixon American participation in the war was de-escalated, and there was a cease-fire January 27, 1973. All American troops were pulled out by March 29.

LESSON XXIII

A TYPICAL STATE

California is the third largest state in the United States. It has a total land area of 155,562 square miles. The distance from north to south, through the center of the state, is 750 miles. The length of the coast line is about 1000 miles.

The state has two parallel mountain systems, extending northwest and southeast, and enclosing between them very broad valleys.

The Coast Range extends throughout the entire state. Among the highest peaks are San Bernardino Mountain, 10,603 feet; San Jacinto, 10,805 feet, and Tehachapi, 9,214 feet.

East of the Coast Range is the rugged Sierra Nevada. In these ranges are Mount Whitney, 14,502 feet, and Mount Shasta, 14,380 feet.

No other state — indeed few countries in the world — can boast of so delightful a climate as that of the valley lands of California. Two seasons, the wet and the dry, divide the year. The average rainfall for the entire state is twenty-three inches. Snow seldom falls except in the mountains, and flowers bloom in the gardens at Christmas time.

The first white people to enter California were Spaniards, who visited the Santa Barbara coast in 1542. In 1579 Sir Francis Drake, an Englishman, explored the coast northward toward San Francisco Bay. Later, other navigators explored the bays of San Diego and Monterey.

In 1769 the Franciscan fathers established the first mission, at San Diego. San Francisco was founded in 1776. By 1823, twenty-one missions had been established, extending as far north as Sonoma.

California was at first a colony of Spain. It became part of the territory of Mexico in 1822. The first American immigration wagon train came in 1826. Others soon followed.

In 1840 Monterey was made the capital. Trouble arose between settlers who wished annexation to the United States and those who wished to remain under Mexican rule. When the United States was preparing to go to war with Mexico, in 1846, a party of Americans, headed by John C. Fremont, seized the town of Sonoma, raised the Bear Flag, and proclaimed the independence of California. Commodore Sloat shortly afterward seized Monterey and San Francisco. On February 2, 1848, by the terms of the treaty with Mexico, California became part of the United States.

In 1848 gold was discovered in Sutter's Creek. Immigration at once set in from all sections of the United States and from European countries. By the close of 1849 there were 100,000 people in California.

On September 9, 1850, California was admitted into the Union. Slavery was forbidden by the state constitution.

California has grown steadily and rapidly in population and in prosperity. It is one of the foremost states educationally in the Union.

The population of California on July 1, 1980 was 23,668,562. The total population in 1970 was 20,980,863.

The fifty-eight counties of California are the following: Alameda, Alpine, Amador, Calaveras, Butte, Colusa, Contra Costa, Del Norte, El Dorado, Fresno, Glenn, Humboldt, Imperial, Inyo, Kern, Kings, Lake, Lassen, Los Angeles, Madera, Marin, Mariposa, Mendocino, Merced, Modoc, Mono, Monterey, Napa, Nevada, Orange, Placer, Plumas, Riverside, Sacramento, San Benito, San Bernardino, Santa Clara, San Diego, San Francisco, San Joaquin, San Luis Obispo, San Mateo, Santa Barbara, Santa Cruz, Shasta, Sierra, Siskiyou, Solano, Sonoma, Stanislaus, Sutter, Tehama, Trinity, Tulare, Tuolumne, Ventura, Yolo, Yuba.

CALIFORNIA STATE GOVERNMENT

The California Legislature consists of two houses called the Senate and the Assembly. There are forty State Senators in the Senate and eighty Assemblymen in the Assembly. They are elected by districts and must reside in the districts which they represent.

The California Legislature meets in regular sessions each January at Sacramento, the State Capital. Special sessions can be called by the Governor at any time to consider an important current problem.

If the Governor of California vetoes a bill it may be passed over his veto by a two-thirds majority of both houses of the legislature.

If the Governor keeps the bill ten days, it becomes a law unless the ten days are at the close of a session. The Governor is allowed thirty days after the close of a legislative session to sign bills.

The Lieutenant Governor presides over the Senate and a Speaker, elected by the Assemblymen, presides over the Assembly.

AMENDMENTS

An amendment to the California Constitution may be proposed in either house of the legislature. If passed by both houses by a two-thirds majority vote, the amendment is submitted to the people. If a majority of the votes cast are in favor of the amendment, it becomes part of the constitution.

THE INITIATIVE, THE REFERENDUM AND THE RECALL

California and several other states have introduced some modern features in legislation. Among these are the initiative, the referendum, and the recall.

The Initiative: Usually laws originate in one of the two houses of the legislature. By the initiative system, voters may propose a law by means of a petition and if a sufficient number of voters sign the petition the proposed law may be placed on the ballot to be voted upon directly by the people. Initiative petitions secured the placing on the ballot, November, 1966, of a measure commonly called "The Anti Obscenity Law." This initiative measure was defeated by the voters. The basis for the defeat appeared to be several legal opinions that the measure, as written, was probably unconstitutional.

The Referendum: If the legislature passes a law which some of the voters do not like, referendum petitions may be circulated, asking that the law may not go into effect until the people have voted upon it. If the required number of voters sign the petition, the law is deferred, and is placed upon the ballot at the next state election. If a majority of the votes are against it at the election, the law does not go into effect.

The Recall: If citizens are not satisfied with a public officer whom they have elected, they may circulate petitions calling for an election to dismiss this officer and put someone else in his place. The recall has been invoked many times in California, and has been successful in some instances.

The initiative, the referendum, and the recall are considered measures tending to greater democracy, as in each case the wishes of the majority of the voters prevail. They are slower and more expensive than the ordinary methods. They are, however, considered a very good check on extravagance or favoritism on the part of officials.

QUESTIONS

1. *Q.* Where and when does the California legislature meet?
   A. The legislature meets at Sacramento, in January, every year.
2. *Q.* Who presides over the Senate in California?
   A. The Lieutenant Governor presides over the Senate.

3. *Q.* Who presides over the Assembly?
    A. The Speaker presides over the Assembly.
4. *Q.* How many members are there in each house?
    A. There are forty members in the State Senate and eighty in the Assembly.
5. *Q.* What is the term of office of members of the legislature?
    A. The term of office of State Senators is four years, and of Assembly-men two years.
6. *Q.* How is the California Constitution amended?
    A. An amendment must be passed by a two-thirds majority vote of both houses of the legislature and must then be ratified by a majority vote of the people.
7. *Q.* Has the California Constitution ever been amended?
    A. Yes, the state constitution has a great number of amendments. Several amendments are passed by the legislature at each regular session, and submitted to the voters at the next state election. Comparatively few of these receive a majority vote of the people.
8. *Q.* What are some of the amendments to the California state constitution?
    A. Amendments have brought into the California state constitution the initiative, referendum, and recall; the present regulations in regard to primary elections; the establishment of the Public Utilities Commission; the workmen's compensation provisions; civil service requirements for state employees; the present method of electing judges of appellate courts; the provisions requiring the sale of food where liquor is sold for consumption. Fewer amendments have been made during recent years.

    At the election of November 7, 1946, the voters ratified an amendment which provides that the state legislature shall meet every year, instead of every second year.
9. *Q.* What is the initiative?
    A. The initiative is a method by which laws and some amendments originate with the voters instead of in the legislature, and are voted upon by the people.
10. *Q.* What is the referendum?
    A. The referendum is a method by which the voters are given an opportunity to determine whether a law passed by the legislature should go into effect.
11. *Q.* What is the recall?
    A. The recall is a method by which an unsatisfactory officer may be removed from office and another officer substituted, through an election.

LESSON XXIV

IMPORTANT OFFICIALS OF CALIFORNIA
FROM—ROSTER OF CALIFORNIA OFFICIALS

Pete Wilson, Governor
Leo T. McCarthy, Lieutenant Governor
March K. Fong Eu, Secretary of State
Kathleen Brown, Treasurer
Dan Lungren, Attorney General
Gray Davis, Controller
Bill Honig, Superintendent of Public Instruction

STATE BOARD OF EQUALIZATION

William Bennett, First District.........................Northern California
Brad Sherman, Second District..........................Central Coast
Ernest Dronenberg, Third District ....Southern California
Matt Fong, Fourth District...............................Los Angeles

GOVERNOR'S CABINET

Lieutenant Governor, Secretary of State, Executive Assistant to the Governor, State Controller, State Treasurer, Attorney General, Superintendent of Public Instruction, Secretary of Business and Transportation, Secretary of Resources, Director of the Department of Finance, Secretary of the Department of Health and Welfare, Secretary of Agriculture and Services.

STATE SUPREME COURT

Chief Justice—Malcolm Lucas.

Associate Justices—Judges Stanley Mosk, Allen Broussard, Edward Panelli, Joyce Kennard, Armand Arabian, and Marvin Baxter.

(The Supreme Court holds sessions in Sacramento, San Francisco, and Los Angeles.)

STATE COURT OF APPEALS

San Francisco—First District
Los Angeles—Second District
Sacramento—Third District
San Diego—Fourth District
Fresno—Fifth District
San Jose—Sixth District

UNITED STATES DISTRICT COURTS (CALIFORNIA)

Central District—Los Angeles
Eastern District—Sacramento and Fresno
Southern District—San Diego
Northern District—San Francisco

UNITED STATES SENATORS

Alan Cranston, elected in 1968.
John Seymour, appointed in 1991.

MEMBERS OF THE HOUSE OF REPRESENTATIVES

District No. 1—Frank Riggs (R)
District No. 2—Wally Herger (R)
District No. 3—Robert T. Matsui (D)
District No. 4—Vic Fazio (D)
District No. 5—Nancy Pelosi (D)
District No. 6—Barbara Boxer (D)
District No. 7—George Miller (D)
District No. 8—Ronald V. Dellums (D)
District No. 9—Fortney Stark (D)
District No. 10—Don Edwards (D)
District No. 11—Tom Lantos (D)
District No. 12—Tom Campbell (R)
District No. 13—Norman Y. Mineta (D)
District No. 14—John T. Doolittle (R)
District No. 15—Gary A. Condit (D)
District No. 16—Leon Panetta (D)
District No. 17—Calvin Dooley (D)
District No. 18—Richard H. Lehman (D)
District No. 19—Robert Lagomarsino (R)
District No. 20—Bill M. Thomas (R)
District No. 21—Elton Gallegly (R)
District No. 22—Carlos Moorhead (R)
District No. 23—Anthony Beilenson (D)
District No. 24—Henry A. Waxman (D)
District No. 25—Edward R. Roybal (D)
District No. 26—Howard Berman (D)
District No. 27—Mel Levine (D)
District No. 28—Julian C. Dixon (D)
District No. 29—Maxine Waters (D)
District No. 30—Matt Martinez (D)
District No. 31—Mervyn Dymally (D)
District No. 32—Glenn Anderson (D)
District No. 33—David Dreier (R)
District No. 34—Esteban Torres (D)
District No. 35—Jerry Lewis (R)
District No. 36—George Brown (D)
District No. 37—Al McCandless (R)
District No. 38—Robert K. Dornan (R)
District No. 39—William Dannemeyer (R)
District No. 40—Christopher Cox (R)
District No. 41—Bill Lowery (R)
District No. 42—Dana Rohrabacher (R)
District No. 43—Ron Packard (R)
District No. 44—Randy Cunningham (R)
District No. 45—Duncan Hunter (R)

LESSON XXV

THE CONSTITUTION
OF THE UNITED STATES OF AMERICA*

WE THE PEOPLE of the United States, in Order to form a more perfect Union, establish Justice, insure domestic Tranquility, provide for the common defense, promote the general Welfare, and secure the Blessings of Liberty to ourselves and our Posterity, do ordain and establish this CONSTITUTION for the United States of America.

ARTICLE I.

SECTION 1. All legislative Powers herein granted shall be vested in a Congress of the United States, which shall consist of a Senate and House of Representatives.

SECTION 2. The House of Representatives shall be composed of Members chosen every second Year by the People of the several States, and the Electors of each State shall have the Qualifications requisite for Electors of the most numerous Branch of the State Legislature.

No person shall be a Representative who shall not have attained to the Age of twenty-five Years, and been seven Years a Citizen of the United States, and who shall not, when elected, be an Inhabitant of that State in which he shall be chosen.

[Representatives and direct Taxes shall be apportioned among the several States which may be included within this Union, according to their respective Numbers, which shall be determined by adding to the whole Number of free Persons, including those bound to Service for a Term of Years, and excluding the Indians not taxed, three fifths of all other Persons.] The actual Enumeration shall be made within three Years after the first Meeting of the Congress of the United States, and within every subsequent Term of ten Years, in such Manner as they shall by Law direct. The Number of Representatives shall not exceed one for every thirty Thousand, but each State shall have at least one Representative; and until such enumeration shall be made, the State of New Hampshire shall be entitled to chuse three, Massachusetts eight, Rhode Island and Providence Plantations one, Connecticut five, New York six, New Jersey four, Pennsylvania eight, Delaware one, Maryland six, Virginia ten, North Carolina five, South Carolina five, and Georgia three.

When vacancies happen in the Representation from any State, the Executive Authority thereof shall issue Writs of Election to fill such Vacancies.

The House of Representatives shall chuse their Speaker and other Officers; and shall have the sole Power of Impeachment.

SECTION 3. The Senate of the United States shall be composed of two Senators from each State, chosen by the Legislature thereof, for six Years; and each Senator shall have one Vote.

Immediately after they shall be assembled in Consequence of the first Election, they shall be divided as equally as may be into three Classes. The Seats of the Senators of the first Class shall be vacated at the Expiration of the second Year, of the second Class at the Expiration of the fourth Year, and of the third Class at the Expiration of the

*The spelling and punctuation used in this copy of the Constitution are the same as those used in the original document.

sixth Year, so that one-third may be chosen every second Year; and if Vacancies happen by Resignation, or otherwise, during the Recess of the Legislature of any State, the Executive thereof may make temporary Appointments until the next Meeting of the Legislature, which shall then fill such Vacancies.

No Person shall be a Senator who shall not have attained to the Age of thirty Years, and been nine Years a Citizen of the United States, and who shall not when elected, be an Inhabitant of that State for which he shall be chosen.

The Vice President of the United States shall be President of the Senate, but shall have no Vote, unless they be equally divided.

The Senate shall chuse their other Officers, and also a President pro tempore, in the absence of the Vice President, or when he shall exercise the Office of President of the United States.

The Senate shall have the sole Power to try all Impeachments. When sitting for that Purpose, they shall be on Oath or Affirmation. When the President of the United States is tried, the Chief Justice shall preside: And no Person shall be convicted without the Concurrence of two thirds of the Members present.

Judgment in Cases of Impeachment shall not extend further than to removal from Office, and disqualification to hold and enjoy any Office of honor, Trust or Profit under the United States: but the Party convicted shall nevertheless be liable and subject to Indictment, Trial, Judgment and Punishment, according to Law.

SECTION 4. The Times, Places and Manner of holding Elections for Senators and Representatives, shall be prescribed in each State by the Legislature thereof: but the Congress may at any time by Law make or alter such Regulations, except as to the Place of Chusing Senators.

The Congress shall assemble at least once in every Year, and such Meeting shall be on the first Monday in December, unless they shall by Law appoint a different Day.

SECTION 5. Each House shall be the Judge of the Elections, Returns and Qualifications of its own Members, and a Majority of each shall constitute a Quorum to do Business; but a smaller Number may adjourn from day to day, and may be authorized to compel the Attendance of absent Members, in such Manner, and under such Penalties as each House may provide.

Each House may determine the Rules of its Proceedings, punish its Members for disorderly Behavior, and, with the Concurrence of two thirds, expel a Member.

Each House shall keep a Journal of its Proceedings, and from time to time publish the same, excepting such Parts as may in their Judgment require Secrecy; and the Yeas and Nays of the Members of either House on any question shall, at the Desire of one fifth of those Present, be entered on the Journal.

Neither House, during the Session of Congress, shall, without the Consent of the other, adjourn for more than three days, nor to any other Place than that in which the two Houses shall be sitting.

SECTION 6. The Senators and Representatives shall receive a Compensation for their services, to be ascertained by Law, and paid out of the Treasury of the United States. They shall in all Cases, except Treason, Felony and Breach of the Peace, be privileged from Arrest during their Attendance at the Session of their respective Houses, and in going to and returning from the same; and for any Speech or Debate in either House, they shall not be questioned in any other Place.

No Senator or Representative shall, during the Time for which he was elected, be appointed to any civil Office under the Authority of the United States, which shall have been created, or the Emoluments whereof shall have been encreased during such time;

and no Person holding any Office under the United States, shall be a Member of either House during his Continuance in Office.

SECTION 7. All Bills for raising Revenue shall originate in the House of Representatives; but the Senate may propose or concur with Amendments as on other Bills.

Every Bill which shall have passed the House of Representatives and the Senate, shall, before it become a Law, be presented to the President of the United States; If he approve he shall sign it, but if not he shall return it, with his Objections to that House in which it shall have originated, who shall enter the Objections at large on their Journal, and proceed to reconsider it. If after such Reconsideration two thirds of that House shall agree to pass the Bill, it shall be sent, together with the Objections, to the other House, by which it shall likewise be reconsidered, and if approved by two thirds of that House, it shall become a Law. But in all such Cases the Votes of both Houses shall be determined by Yeas and Nays, and the Names of the Persons voting for and against the Bill shall be entered on the Journal of each House respectively. If any Bill shall not be returned by the President within ten Days (Sundays excepted), after it shall have been presented to him, the Same shall be a Law, in like Manner as if he had signed it, unless the Congress by their Adjournment prevent its Return, in which Case it shall not be a Law.

Every Order, Resolution, or Vote to which the Concurrence of the Senate and House of Representatives may be necessary (except on a question of Adjournment) shall be presented to the President of the United States; and before the Same shall take Effect, shall be approved by him, or being disapproved by him, shall be repassed by two thirds of the Senate and House of Representatives, according to the Rules and Limitations described in the Case of a Bill.

SECTION 8. The Congress shall have Power To lay and collect Taxes, duties, imposts and Excises, to pay the Debts and provide for the common Defense and general Welfare of the United States; but all Duties, Imposts and Excises shall be uniform throughout the United States;

To borrow money on the credit of the United States;

To regulate Commerce with foreign Nations, and among the several States, and with the Indian Tribes;

To establish an uniform Rule of Naturalization, and uniform Laws on the subject of Bankruptcies throughout the United States.

To coin Money, regulate the Value thereof, and of foreign Coin, and fix the Standard of Weights and Measures.

To provide for the Punishment of counterfeiting the Securities and current Coin of the United States;

To establish Post Offices and post Roads;

To promote the Progress of Science and useful Arts, by securing for limited Times to Authors and Inventors the exclusive Right to their respective Writings and Discoveries;

To constitute Tribunals inferior to the supreme Court;

To define and punish Piracies and Felonies committed on the high Seas, and Offenses against the Law of Nations;

To declare War, grant Letters of Marque and Reprisal, and make Rules concerning Captures on Land and Water;

To raise and support Armies, but no Appropriation of Money to that Use shall be for a longer term than two Years;

To provide and maintain a Navy;

To make Rules for the Government and Regulation of the land and naval forces;

To provide for calling forth the Militia to execute the Laws of the Union, suppress Insurrections and Repel Invasions;

To provide for organizing, arming, and disciplining the Militia, and for governing such Part of them as may be employed in the Service of the United States, reserving to the States respectively, the Appointment of the Officers, and the Authority of training the Militia according to the discipline prescribed by Congress;

To exercise exclusive Legislation in all Cases whatsoever, over such District (not exceeding ten Miles square) as may, by Cession of particular States, and the acceptance of Congress, become the Seat of the Government of the United States, and to exercise like Authority over all places purchased by the Consent of the Legislature of the State in which the Same shall be, for the Erection of Forts, Magazines, Arsenals, dock-Yards, and other needful Buildings; — And

To make all Laws which shall be necessary and proper for carrying into Execution the foregoing Powers, and all other Powers vested by this Constitution in the Government of the United States, or in any Department of Officer thereof.

SECTION 9. The Migration or Importation of such Persons as any of the States now existing shall think proper to admit, shall not be prohibited by the Congress prior to the Year one thousand eight hundred and eight, but a tax or duty may be imposed on such Importation, not exceeding ten dollars for each Person.

The privilege of the Writ of Habeas Corpus shall not be suspended, unless when in Cases of Rebellion or Invasion the public Safety may require it.

No Bill of Attainder or ex post facto Law shall be passed.

No capitation, or other direct, Tax shall be laid, unless in Proportion to the Census or Enumeration herein before directed to be taken.

No Tax or Duty shall be laid on Articles exported from any State.

No Preference shall be given by any Regulation of Commerce or Revenue to the Ports of one State over those of another: nor shall Vessels bound to, or from, one State, be obliged to enter, clear, or pay Duties to another.

No Money shall be drawn from the Treasury, but in Consequence of Appropriations made by Law; and a regular Statement and Account of the Receipts and Expenditures of all public Money shall be published from time to time.

No Title of Nobility shall be granted by the United States: And no Person holding any Office of Profit or Trust under them, shall, without the Consent of the Congress, accept of any present, Emolument, Office, or Title, of any kind whatever, from any King, Prince, or foreign State.

SECTION 10. No State shall enter into any Treaty, Alliance, or Confederation; grant Letters of Marque and Reprisal; coin Money; emit Bills of Credit; make any Thing but gold and silver Coin a Tender in Payment of Debts, pass any Bill of Attainder, ex post facto Law, or Law impairing the Obligation of Contracts, or grant any Title of Nobility.

No State shall, without the Consent of the Congress, lay any imposts or Duties on Imports or Exports, except what may be absolutely necessary for executing its inspection Laws; and the net Produce of all Duties and Imposts, laid by any State on Imports or Exports, shall be for the Use of the Treasury of the United States; and all such Laws shall be subject to the Revision and Controul of the Congress.

No State shall, without the Consent of Congress, lay any duty of Tonnage, keep Troops, or Ships of War in time of Peace, enter into any Agreement or Compact with another State, or with a foreign Power, or engage in War, unless actually invaded, or in such imminent Danger as will not admit of delay.

ARTICLE II.

SECTION 1. The executive Power shall be vested in a President of the United States of America. He shall hold his Office during the Term of four Years, and, together with the Vice-President, chosen for the same Term, be elected as follows:

Each State shall appoint, in such Manner as the Legislature thereof may direct, a Number of Electors, equal to the whole Number of Senators and Representatives to which the State may be entitled in Congress: but no Senator or Representative, or Person holding an Office of Trust or Profit under the United States, shall be appointed an Elector.

[The Electors shall meet in their respective State, and vote by Ballot for two persons, of whom one at least shall not be an Inhabitant of the same State with themselves. And they shall make a List of all the Persons voted for, and of the Number of Votes for each; which List they shall sign and certify, and transmit sealed to the Seat of the Government of the United States, directed to the President of the Senate. The President of the Senate shall, in the Presence of the Senate and House of Representatives, open all the Certificates, and the Votes shall then be counted. The Person having the greatest Number of Votes shall then be the President, if such Number be a Majority of the whole Number of Electors appointed; and if there be more than one who have such Majority, and have an equal Number of Votes, then the House of Representatives shall immediately chuse by Ballot one of them for President; and if no Person have a Majority, then from the five highest on the List the said House shall in like Manner chuse the President. But in chusing the President, the Votes shall be taken by States, the Representation for each State having one Vote; A quorum for this purpose shall consist of a Member or Members from two-thirds of the States, and a Majority of all the States shall be necessary to a Choice. In every Case, after the Choice of the President, the Person having the greatest Number of Votes of the Electors shall be the Vice President. But if there should remain two or more who have equal Votes, the Senate shall chuse from them by Ballot the Vice President.]

The Congress may determine the Time of Chusing the Electors, and the Day on which they shall give their Votes; which Day shall be the same throughout the United States.

No person except a natural born Citizen, or a Citizen of the United States, at the time of the Adoption of this Constitution, shall be eligible to the Office of President; neither shall any Person be eligible to that Office who shall not have attained to the Age of thirty-five Years, and been fourteen Years a Resident within the United States.

In Case of the Removal of the President from Office, or of his Death, Resignation, or Inability to discharge the Powers and Duties of the said Office, the same shall devolve on the Vice President, and the Congress may by Law provide for the Case of Removal, Death, Resignation or Inability, both of the President and Vice President, declaring what Officer shall then act as President, and such Officer shall act accordingly, until the Disability be removed, or a President shall be elected.

The President shall, at stated Times, receive for his Services, a Compensation, which shall neither be encreased nor diminished during the Period for which he shall have been elected, and he shall not receive within that Period any other Emolument from the United States, or any of them.

Before he enter on the Execution of his Office, he shall take the following Oath or Affirmation: — "I do solemnly swear (or affirm) that I will faithfully execute the Office of President of the United States, and will to the best of my Ability, preserve, protect and defend the Constitution of the United States."

SECTION 2. The President shall be Commander in Chief of the Army and Navy of the United States, and of the Militia of the several States, when called into the actual Service of the United States; he may require the Opinion in writing, of the principal Officer in each of the executive Departments, upon any subject relating to the Duties of their respective Offices, and he shall have Power to Grant Reprieves and Pardons for Offenses against the United States, except in Cases of Impeachment.

He shall have Power, by and with the Advice and Consent of the Senate, to make Treaties, provided two-thirds of the Senators present concur; and he shall nominate, and by and with the Advice and Consent of the Senate, shall appoint Ambassadors, other public Ministers and Consuls, Judges of the supreme Court, and all other Officers of the United States, whose Appointments are not herein otherwise provided for, and which shall be established by Law; but the Congress may by Law vest the Appointment of such inferior Officers, as they think proper, in the President alone, in the Courts of Law, or in the Heads of Departments.

The President shall have Power to fill up all Vacancies that may happen during the Recess of the Senate, by granting Commissions which shall expire at the End of their next Session.

SECTION 3. He shall from time to time give to the Congress Information of the State of the Union, and recommend to their Consideration such Measures as he shall judge necessary and expedient; he may, on extraordinary Occasions, convene both Houses, or either of them, and in Case of Disagreement between them, with Respect to the Time of Adjournment, he may adjourn them to such Time as he shall think proper; he shall receive Ambassadors and other public Ministers; he shall take Care that the Laws be faithfully executed, and shall Commission all the Officers of the United States.

SECTION 4. The President, Vice President and all civil Officers of the United States, shall be removed from Office on Impeachment for, and Conviction of, Treason, Bribery, or other high Crimes and Misdemeanors.

ARTICLE III.

SECTION 1. The judicial Power of the United States, shall be vested in one supreme Court, and in such inferior Courts as the Congress may from time to time ordain and establish. The Judges, both of the supreme and inferior Courts, shall hold their Offices during good Behaviour, and shall, at stated Times, receive for their Services a Compensation which shall not be diminished during their Continuance in Office.

SECTION 2. The judicial Power shall extend to all Cases, in Law and Equity, arising under this Constitution, the Laws of the United States, and Treaties made, or which shall be made, under their Authority; — to all Cases affecting Ambassadors, other public Ministers and Consuls; — to all Cases of admiralty and maritime Jurisdiction; — to Controversies to which the United States shall be a party; — to Controversies between two or more States — between a State and Citizens of another State; — between Citizens of different States; — between Citizens of the same State claiming Lands under Grants of different States, and between a State, or the Citizens thereof, and foreign States, Citizens or Subjects.

In all Cases affecting Ambassadors, other public Ministers and Consuls, and those in which a State shall be Party, the supreme Court shall have original Jurisdiction. In all other Cases before mentioned, the supreme Court shall have appellate Jurisdiction, both as to Law and Fact, with such Exceptions, and under such Regulations as the Congress shall make.

The trial of all Crimes, except in Cases of Impeachment, shall be by Jury; and such Trial shall be held in the State where the said Crimes shall have been committed; but when not committed within any State, the Trial shall be at such Place or Places as the Congress may by Law have directed.

SECTION 3. Treason against the United States, shall consist only in levying War against them, or in adhering to their Enemies, giving them Aid and Comfort. No person shall be convicted of Treason unless on the Testimony of two Witnesses to the same overt Act, or on Confession in open Court.

The Congress shall have power to declare the Punishment of Treason, but no Attainder of Treason shall work Corruption of Blood, or Forfeiture except during the life of the Person attainted.

ARTICLE IV.

SECTION 1. Full Faith and Credit shall be given in each State to the public Acts, Records, and judicial Proceedings of every other State. And the Congress may by general Laws prescribe the Manner in which such Acts, Records and Proceedings shall be proved, and the Effect thereof.

SECTION 2. The Citizens of each State shall be entitled to all Privileges and Immunities of Citizens in the several States.

A Person charged in any State with Treason, Felony, or other Crime, who shall flee from Justice, and be found in another State, shall on demand of the executive Authority of the State from which he fled, be delivered up, to be removed to the State having Jurisdiction of the Crime.

No Person held to Service of Labour in one State, under the Laws thereof, escaping into another, shall, in Consequence of any Law or Regulation therein, be discharged from such Service or Labour, but shall be delivered up on Claim of the Party to whom such Service or Labour may be due.

SECTION 3. New States may be admitted by the Congress into this Union; but no new State shall be formed or erected within the Jurisdiction of any other State; nor any State be formed by the Junction of two or more States, or parts of States, without the Consent of the Legislatures of the States concerned as well as of the Congress.

The Congress shall have Power to dispose of and make all needful Rules and Regulations respecting the Territory or other Property belonging to the United States; and nothing in this Constitution shall be so construed as to Prejudice any Claims of the United States, or of any particular State.

SECTION 4. The United States shall guarantee to every State in this Union a Republican Form of Government, and shall protect each of them against Invasion; and on Application of the Legislature, or of the Executive (when the Legislature cannot be convened) against domestic Violence.

ARTICLE V.

The Congress, whenever two-thirds of both Houses shall deem it necessary, shall propose Amendments to this Constitution, or, on the Application of the Legislatures of two-thirds of the several States, shall call a Convention for proposing Amendments, which, in either Case, shall be valid to all Intents and Purposes, as part of this Constitution, when ratified by the Legislatures of three-fourths of the several States, or by Conventions in three-fourths thereof, as the one or the other Mode of Ratification may be proposed by the Congress; Provided that no Amendment which may be made prior to the Year One thousand eight hundred and eight shall in any Manner affect the first and fourth Clauses in the Ninth Section of the first Article; and that no State, without its Consent, shall be deprived of its equal Suffrage in the Senate.

ARTICLE VI.

All Debts contracted and Engagements entered into, before the Adoption of this Constitution, shall be as valid against the United States under this Constitution, as under the Confederation.

This Constitution, and the Laws of the United States which shall be made in Pursuance thereof; and all Treaties made, or which shall be made, under the Authority of the United States, shall be the supreme Law of the Land; and the Judges in every State shall be bound thereby, any Thing in the Constitution or Laws of any State to the Contrary notwithstanding.

The Senators and Representatives before mentioned, and the Members of the several State Legislatures, and all executive and judicial Officers, both of the United States and of the several States, shall be bound by Oath or Affirmation, to support this Constitution; but no religious Test shall ever be required as a Qualification to any Office or public Trust under the United States.

ARTICLE VII.

The Ratification of the Conventions of nine States shall be sufficient for the Establishment of this Constitution between the States so ratifying Same.

DONE in Convention by the Unanimous Consent of the States present the Seventeenth Day of September in the Year of our Lord one thousand seven hundred and Eighty seven and of the Independence of the United States of America the Twelfth. In Witness whereof We have hereunto subscribed our Names

(Signatures of representatives of the participating States)

ARTICLES in Addition to, and Amendment Of, the Constitution of the United States of America, Proposed by Congress, and Ratified by the Legislatures of the Several States, Pursuant to the Fifth Article of the Original Constitution.

[ARTICLE I.]

Congress shall make no law respecting an establishment of religion, or prohibiting the free exercise thereof; or abridging the freedom of speech, or of the press; or the right of the people peaceably to assemble, and to petition the Government for a redress of grievances.

[ARTICLE II.]

A well regulated Militia, being necessary to the security of a free State, the right of the people to keep and bear Arms, shall not be infringed.

[ARTICLE III.]

No Soldier shall, in time of peace be quartered in any house, without the consent of the Owner, nor in time of war, but in a manner to be prescribed by law.

[ARTICLE IV.]

The right of the people to be secure in their persons, houses, papers, and effects, against unreasonable searches and seizures, shall not be violated, and no Warrants shall issue, but upon probable cause, supported by Oath or affirmation, and particularly describing the place to be searched, and the persons or things to be seized.

[ARTICLE V.]

No person shall be held to answer for a capital, or otherwise infamous crime, unless on a presentment or indictment of a Grand Jury, except in cases arising in the land or naval forces, or in the Militia, when in actual service in time of War or public danger; nor shall any person be subject for the same offense to be twice put in jeopardy of life or limb; nor shall be compelled in any criminal case to be a witness against himself nor be deprived of life, liberty, or property, without due process of law; nor shall private property be taken for public use, without just compensation.

[ARTICLE VI.]

In all criminal prosecutions, the accused shall enjoy the right to a speedy and public trial, by an impartial jury of the State and district wherein the crime shall have been committed, which district shall have been previously ascertained by law, and to be informed of the nature and cause of the accusation; to be confronted with the witnesses against him; to have compulsory process for obtaining witnesses in his favor; and to have the Assistance of Counsel for his defense.

[ARTICLE VII.]

In suits at common law, where the value in controversy shall exceed twenty dollars, the right of trial by jury shall be preserved, and no fact tried by a jury, shall be otherwise reexamined in any Court of the United States, than according to the rules of the common law.

[ARTICLE VIII.]

Excessive bail shall not be required, nor excessive fines imposed, nor cruel and unusual punishments inflicted.

[ARTICLE IX.]

The enumeration in the Constitution, of certain rights, shall not. be construed to deny or disparage others retained by the people.

[ARTICLE X.]

The powers not delegated to the United States by the Constitution, nor prohibited by it to the States, are reserved to the States respectively, or to the people.

ARTICLE XI.

The Judicial power of the United States shall not be construed to extend to any suit in law or equity, commenced or prosecuted against one of the United States by Citizens of another State, or by Citizens or Subjects of any Foreign State.

ARTICLE XII.

The Electors shall meet in their respective states and vote by ballot for President and Vice-President, one of whom, at least, shall not be an inhabitant of the same state with themselves; they shall name in their ballots the person voted for as President, and in distinct ballots the person voted for as Vice-President, and they shall make distinct lists of all persons voted for as President, and of all persons voted for as Vice-President, and of the number of votes for each, which lists they shall sign and certify, and transmit sealed to the seat of the government of the United States, directed to the President of the Senate; — The President of the Senate shall, in presence of the Senate and House of Representatives, open all the certificates and the votes shall then be counted; — The person having the greatest number of votes for President, shall be the President, if such number be a majority of the whole number of Electors appointed; and if no person have such majority, then from the persons having the highest numbers not exceeding three on the list of those voted for as President, the House of Representatives shall choose immediately, by ballot, the President. But in choosing the President, the votes shall be taken by states, the representation from each state having one vote; a quorum for this purpose shall consist of a member or members from two-thirds of the states, and a majority of all the states shall be necessary to a choice. And if the House of Representatives shall not choose a President whenever the right of choice shall devolve upon them, before the fourth day of March next following, then the Vice-President shall act as President, as in the case of the death or other constitutional disability of the President. — The person having the greatest number of votes as Vice-President, shall be the Vice-President, if such number be a majority of the whole number of Electors appointed, and if no person have a majority, then from the two highest numbers on the list, the Senate shall choose the Vice-President; a quorum for the purpose shall consist of two-thirds of the whole number of Senators, and a majority of the whole number shall be necessary to a choice. But no person constitutionally ineligible to the office of President shall be eligible to that of Vice-President of the United States.

ARTICLE XIII.

SECTION 1. Neither slavery nor involuntary servitude, except as a punishment for crime whereof the party shall have been duly convicted, shall exist within the United States, or any place subject to their jurisdiction.

SECTION 2. Congress shall have power to enforce this article by appropriate legislation.

ARTICLE XIV.

SECTION 1. All persons born or naturalized in the United States, and subject to the jurisdiction thereof, are citizens of the United States and of the State wherein they reside. No State shall make or enforce any law which shall abridge the privileges or immunities of citizens of the United States; nor shall any State deprive any person of life, liberty, or property, without due process of law; nor deny to any person within its jurisdiction the equal protection of the laws.

SECTION 2. Representatives shall be apportioned among the several States according to their respective numbers, counting the whole numbers of persons in each State, excluding Indians not taxed. But when the right to vote at any election for the choice of electors for President and Vice-President of the United States, Representatives in Congress, the Executive and Judicial officers of a State, or the members of the Legislature thereof, is denied to any of the male inhabitants of such State, being twenty-one years of age, and citizens of the United States, or in any way abridged, except for participation in rebellion, or other crime, the basis of representation therein shall be reduced in the proportion which the number of such male citizens shall bear to the whole number of male citizens twenty-one years of age in such State.

SECTION 3. No person shall be a Senator or Representative in Congress, or elector of President and Vice-President, or hold any office, civil or military, under the United States, or under any State, who, having previously taken an oath, as a member of Congress, or as an officer of the United States, or as a member of any State legislature, or as an executive or judicial officer of any State, to support the Constitution of the United States, shall have engaged in insurrection or rebellion against the same, or given aid or comfort to the enemies thereof. But Congress may by a vote of two-thirds of each House, remove such disability.

SECTION 4. The validity of the public debt of the United States, authorized by law, including debts incurred for payment of pensions and bounties for services in suppressing insurrection or rebellion, shall not be questioned. But neither the United States nor any State shall assume or pay any debt of obligation incurred in aid of insurrection or rebellion against the United States, or any claim for the loss or emancipation of any slave; but all such debts, obligations and claims shall be held illegal and void.

SECTION 5. The Congress shall have the power to enforce, by appropriate legislation, the provisions of this article.

ARTICLE XV.

SECTION 1. The right of citizens of the United States to vote shall not be denied or abridged by the United States or by any State on account of race, color, or previous condition of servitude —

SECTION 2. The Congress shall have power to enforce this article by appropriate legislation.

ARTICLE XVI.

The Congress shall have power to lay and collect taxes on incomes, from whatever source derived, without apportionment among the several States, and without regard to any census or enumeration.

ARTICLE XVII.

The Senate of the United States shall be composed of two Senators from each State, elected by the people thereof, for six years; and each Senator shall have one vote. The electors in each State shall have the qualifications requisite for electors of the most numerous branch of the State legislatures.

When vacancies happen in the representation of any State in the Senate, the executive authority of such State shall issue writs of election to fill such vacancies: *Provided,* That the legislature of any State may empower the executive thereof to make temporary appointments until the people fill the vacancies by election as the legislature may direct.

This amendment shall not be so construed as to affect the election or term of any Senator chosen before it becomes valid as part of the Constitution.

ARTICLE XVIII.

SECTION 1. After one year from the ratification of this article the manufacture, sale, or transportation of intoxicating liquors within, the importation thereof into, or the exportation thereof from the United States and all territory subject to the jurisdiction thereof for beverage purposes is hereby prohibited.

SECTION 2. The Congress and the several States shall have concurrent power to enforce this article by appropriate legislation.

SECTION 3. This article shall be inoperative unless it shall have been ratified as an amendment to the Constitution by the legislatures of the several States, as provided in the Constitution, within seven years from the date of the submission hereof to the States by the Congress.

ARTICLE XIX.

The right of citizens of the United States to vote shall not be denied or abridged by the United States or by any State on account of sex.

Congress shall have power to enforce this article by appropriate legislation.

ARTICLE XX.

SECTION 1. The terms of the President and Vice President shall end at noon on the 20th day of January, and the terms of Senators and Representatives at noon on the 3rd day of January, of the years in which such terms would have ended if this article had not been ratified; and the terms of their successors shall then begin.

SECTION 2. The Congress shall assemble at least once in every year, and such meeting shall begin at noon on the 3rd day of January, unless they shall by law appoint a different day.

SECTION 3. If, at the time fixed for the beginning of the term of the President, the President elect shall have died, the Vice President elect shall become President. If a President shall not have been chosen before the time fixed for the beginning of his term, or if the President elect shall have failed to quality, then the Vice President elect shall act as President until a President shall have qualified; and the Congress may by law provide for the case wherein neither a President elect nor a Vice President elect shall have qualified, declaring who shall then act as President, or the manner in which one who is to act shall be selected, and such person shall act accordingly until a President or Vice President shall have qualified.

SECTION 4. The Congress may by law provide for the case of the death of any of the persons from whom the House of Representatives may choose a President whenever the right of choice shall have devolved upon them, and for the case of the death of any of the persons from whom the Senate may choose a Vice President whenever the right of choice shall have devolved upon them.

SECTION 5. Sections 1 and 2 shall take effect on the 15th day of October following the ratification of this article.

SECTION 6. This article shall be inoperative unless it shall have been ratified as an amendment to the Constitution by the legislatures of three-fourths of the several States within seven years from the date of its submission.

ARTICLE XXI.

SECTION 1. The eighteenth article of amendment to the Constitution of the United States is hereby repealed.

SECTION 2. The transportation or importation into any State, Territory, or possession of the United States for delivery or use therein of intoxicating liquors, in violation of the laws thereof, is hereby prohibited.

SECTION 3. This article shall be inoperative unless it shall have been ratified as an amendment to the Constitution by conventions in the several States, as provided in the Constitution, within seven years from the date of the submission hereof to the States by the Congress.

ARTICLE XXII.

SECTION 1. No person shall be elected to the office of the President more than twice, and no person who has held the office of President, or acted as President, for more than two years of a term to which some other person was elected President shall be elected to the office of the President more than once. But this Article shall not apply to any person holding the office of President when this Article was proposed by the Congress, and shall not prevent any person who may be holding the office of President, or acting as President, during the term within which this Article becomes operative from holding the office of President or acting as President during the remainder of such term.

SECTION 2. This article shall be inoperative unless it shall have been ratified as an amendment to the Constitution by the Legislatures of three-fourths of the several States within seven years from the date of its submission to the States by the Congress.

ARTICLE XXIII.

SECTION 1. The District constituting the seat of government of the United States shall appoint in such manner as the Congress may direct:

A number of electors of President and Vice President equal to the whole number of Senators and Representatives in Congress to which the District would be entitled if it were a State, but in no event more than the least populous state; they shall be in addition to those appointed by the states, but they shall be considered, for the purposes of the election of President and Vice President, to be electors appointed by a state; and they shall meet in the District and perform such duties as provided by the twelfth article of amendment.

SECTION 2. The Congress shall have power to enforce this article by appropriate legislation.

ARTICLE XXIV.

SECTION 1. The right of citizens of the United States to vote in any primary or other election for President or Vice-President, or for Senator or Representative in Congress, shall not be denied or abridged by the United States or any State by reason of failure to pay any poll tax or other tax.

SECTION 2. The Congress shall have power to enforce this article by appropriate legislation.

ARTICLE XXV.

SECTION 1. In case of the removal of the President from office or of his death or resignation, the Vice President shall become President.

SECTION 2. Whenever there is a vacancy in the office of the Vice President, the President shall nominate a Vice President who shall take office upon confirmation by a majority vote of both Houses of Congress.

SECTION 3. Whenever the President transmits to the President *pro tempore* of the Senate and the Speaker of the House of Representatives his written declaration that he is unable to discharge the powers and duties of his office, and until he transmits to them a written declaration to the contrary, such powers and duties shall be discharged by the Vice President as Acting President.

SECTION 4. Whenever the Vice President and a majority of either the principal officers of the executive departments or of such other body as Congress may by law provide, transmit to the President *pro tempore* of the Senate and the Speaker of the House of Representatives their written declaration that the President is unable to discharge the powers and duties of his office, the Vice President shall immediately assume the powers and duties of the office as Acting President.

Thereafter, when the President transmits to the President *pro tempore* of the Senate and the Speaker of the House of Representatives his written declaration that no inability exists, he shall resume the powers and duties of his office unless the Vice President and a majority of either the principal officers of the executive departments or of such other body as Congress may by law provide, transmit within four days to the President *pro tempore* of the Senate and the Speaker of the House of Representatives their written declaration that the President is unable to discharge the powers and duties of his office. Thereupon Congress shall decide the issue, assembling within forty-eight hours for that purpose if not in session. If the Congress, within twenty-one days after receipt of the latter written declaration, or, if Congress is not in session, within twenty-one days after Congress is required to assemble, determines by two-thirds vote of both Houses that the President is unable to discharge the powers and duties of his office, the Vice President shall continue to discharge the same as Acting President; otherwise, the President shall resume the powers and duties of his office.

ARTICLE XXVI.

SECTION 1. The right of citizens of the United States, who are eighteen years of age or older, to vote shall not be denied or abridged by the United States or by any State on account of age.

SECTION 2. The Congress shall have power to enforce this article by appropriate legislation.